# BORDER ⁓ALLADS

JAMES REED was born and brought up in Northumberland. He is the author of *The Border Ballads* (1973) and *Walter Scott: Landscape and Locality* (1980), and the editor of Walter Scott's *Selected Poems* in the FyfieldBooks series.

# Border Ballads

## A Selection

Edited with an introduction by
**JAMES REED**

Fyfield*Books*

**CARCANET**

First published in Great Britain in 1991 by
Carcanet Press Limited
Alliance House
Cross Street
Manchester M2 7AQ

in association with MidNAG
Ashington
Northumberland NE63 8RX

This impression 2003

A CIP catalogue record for this book is available from the British Library
ISBN 1 85754 710 1

The publisher acknowledges financial assistance from Arts Council England

Printed and bound in England by SRP Ltd, Exeter

Mopsa: Pray now buy some. I love a ballet in print,
a life, for then we are sure they are true.

*The Winter's Tale*

# Contents

BALLADS OF THE SUPERNATURAL

# Introduction

BORDER BALLADS belong to a period, a place and its people. Their distinction lies in the interaction of all three of these factors; we diminish them if we see them merely as songs, or merely as poems, without taking into account the environment in which they flourished.

Sir Philip Sidney's famous passage in praise of 'Chevy Chase', 'I never heard the olde song of *Percy* and *Duglas* that I found not my heart mooved more then with a trumpet; and yet it is sung but by some blinde Crouder', is the response of a courtly soldier, but such immediacy was soon lost to more conventionally educated minds, and by the beginning of the eighteenth century we find ballads condescingly regarded as sub-literary verse.

Where Sidney writes of listening to a minstrel, Joseph Addison in two *Spectator* essays (1711) on a later broadside version of the same narrative, writes: 'I must only caution the Reader not to let the simplicity of the Stile, which one may well pardon in so old a Poet, prejudice him against the Greatness of the Thought.' This view of ballads as primitive poems led Bishop Thomas Percy (1729-1811) and his contemporaries to offer 'improved versions', in which the taste of English metropolitan literary scholarship was imposed on regional, often very local, language and style. The research of such musicians as Cecil Sharp (1859-1924), later fieldwork, and the folk revival of the mid-twentieth century have restored the identity of the ballads as songs, and excellent recordings are now available. But awareness of literary style and the pleasure of musical rendering are not enough; the full appreciation of Border Ballads remains incomplete without some knowledge of the terrain to which they are native, and of the way of life of the Borderers who recorded their past in this form.

Sir Walter Scott was the first collector and editor of Border Ballads to reflect seriously, both as historian and man of letters, on the relevance in these songs of place names, family and to-names, history and tradition within a specific region characterized by its own vocabulary, laws and social structure. His

9

*Minstrelsy of the Scottish Border* (1802, 1803) is valuable mainly because of his intense and far-reaching appreciation of Borders and Borderers in the context of local history and custom. In the Introduction to his edition of *Sir Tristrem* (1804) he wrote, 'Tradition depends upon locality. The scene of a celebrated battle, the ruins of an ancient tower, the "historic stone" over the grave of a hero, the hill and valley inhabited of old by a particular tribe, remind posterity of events which are sometimes recorded in their very names'.

In the following year his *Lay of the Last Minstrel* was severely dismissed in a review by Francis Jeffrey whose words accurately reflect contemporary literary taste which, under Scott's influence, was soon to change:

> We really cannot so far sympathise with the local partialities of the author as to feel any glow of patriotism or ancient virtue in hearing of the Todrig or Johnston clans or of Elliots, Armstrongs and Tinlinns; still less can we relish the introduction of Black John of Athelstane, Whitslade the Hawk, Arthur-fire-the-Braes, Red Roland Forster, or any other of those worthies who
>
> > Sought the beeves that made their broth
> > In Scotland and in England both
>
> into a poem which has any pretensions to seriousness or dignity. The ancient metrical romance might have admitted those homely personalities, but the present age will not endure them; and Mr Scott must either sacrifice his Border prejudices, or offend all his readers in other parts of the empire.

These words were written when Scott was little more than a provincial lawyer with literary inclinations, years before he became the most celebrated writer of his time. They would not have appeared exceptional in 1805.

As they have survived in the major printed collections of Scott and Child, Border Ballads bear the marks of severe damage inflicted by time, prejudice, oral transmission and literary distortion. Hence it is unwise to make precise generalizations about structure, and the commentator does well to bear in mind Kipling's lines: 'There are nine and sixty ways of constructing tribal lays / And every single one of them is right!' I concern myself, therefore, in what follows, not with reductive rules, but with general comment on some of the ways in which these ballads achieve their effects.

The key to an appreciation of action, especially in the Riding Ballads, is an awareness of their consistent economy of language and incident. We are rarely called aside by the singer and asked to admire the view, though exceptions do occur, as in the opening stanzas of 'The Outlaw Murray' (p.82), quite untypical in its mild, leisurely description. The outstanding stories of raid and reif open with lines in which the balladist conveys information with a vitality which pitches the audience directly into the action, place and season. The first stanzas of 'Jamie Telfer' (p.75) move from the narrator's brief placing of the event in time to the chief aggressor, the need for a guide and an introductory dialogue. By stanza four the raiders from Bewcastle are assaulting Telfer's pele. Similarly, 'Kinmont Willie' (p.29) opens with a rousing appeal calling distinctive attention to three major characters, 'fause Sakelde', 'keen Lord Scroope', and 'bauld Kinmont'; we know now exactly whose side we are on, and the action begins instantly. 'Hobie Noble' (p.42) begins with an interesting variant, making the first two stanzas a prelude to the tale of violence and treachery by setting a tone of bitter lament over the betrayal of 'brave Noble'.

First-person narrative is rare, though it does play a parenthetical part in 'The Raid of the Reidswire' (p.101); 'Carmichael was our Warden then'; 'Of other clans I cannot tell / Because our warning was not wide'; and a more telling, partisan local one in 'The Battle of Otterburn' (p.107): 'The Perssy was a man of strength, / I tell yow in this stounde'.

But the main thrust in the Riding Ballads comes from dialogue, often dramatically presented in terms of question (or challenge) and response, punctuated by brief narrative movements, both illuminating the regional *mores*, or the Border Law, and driving on the story.

11

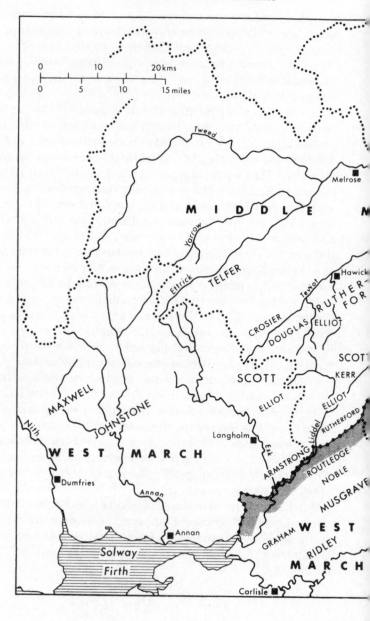

Such elements control pace and tone; most of the normal devices of poetic composition are absent. Ballad narrative is a simple plotless progression; meaning tends to be conveyed through literal, often repetitive statement largely stripped of metaphor and rhetoric. This is what makes the following stanzas from 'Kinmont Willie' stand out as a neat literary fabrication, not a singer's invention:

'O is my basnet a widow's curch?
        Or my lance a wand of the willow tree?
    Or my arm a ladye's lilye hand
        That an English lord should lightly me!'

The action here is frozen while the speaker elaborates cumulatively in figurative terms lines which contrast unfavourably with the compressed power of the ballad's opening.

Romance in the Borders usually spells tragedy, and in the ballads this often finds expression in a blend of violence and lament; family feud cannot separate lovers in life, though it may in death. 'The Douglas Tragedy' (p.121) is an adventurous, murderous love story, employing in its dialogue and in the energy of its unsentimental narrative many characteristics of the Riding Ballad; but its directness is exceptional. Most ballads of Border tragedy achieve their effects through the very obliqueness of their story-telling; the chill of lonely, vengeful death is nowhere more deeply felt than in 'The Twa Corbies' (p.140), a story of passion and treachery conveyed through the dialogue of a pair of carrion crows. Even the fact that their talk is overheard by the narrator introduces an eavesdropping frisson in the opening lines, intensified by the ironic 'making a mane' where their lament takes the form of a discussion of how they will dine on the dead man who has been betrayed by his mistress. Their repast is unlikely to be disturbed by any mourning presence, since the lady is off with her new love: 'His lady's ta'en another mate / So we may mak our dinner sweet.' Such macabre elegance may be due to a literary hand rather than a minstrel tongue, but it is telling in the typical economy of its cool understatement.

14

'Lord Randal' (p.139) too has been murdered by his true love, but she is never directly accused; what lies behind his poisoning is more vividly imagined than stated. The question and answer form is used also in 'Edward' (p.137), where the audience gradually discovers what the mother already knows, in a manner which slowly releases a rage of guilt and hatred in her son. Similarly, 'The Lament of the Border Widow' (p.128) is a monologue in which the actual tragedy is suggested in a spare, unelaborate language. The Border Widow expresses in a mere seven quatrains simultaneous emotions of true love, treachery, bereavement and the lonely responsibilities of widowhood. The widow's burden is a commonplace in the official records of appeals for redress under Border Law. We find it again in 'The Battle of Otterburn':

> Then on the morne they made them beerys
>> Of byrch and haysell gray;
> Many a wydowe, wyth wepyng teyres,
>> Ther makes they fette away.

In all of this there is a bond of common knowledge, common experience, common language. What we have lost over the past four centuries is not the spirit of song or the flash of minstrel invention but the sense of a Border community to whose members these ballads were both fact and romance, history and entertainment. Family names that crossed the singer's lips were their names, his places their places, his loyalties theirs. Singer and song remain; print, education, social mobility and peace have done for the rest.

Border Ballads form part of our record of the world of those who lived, long before the present political boundaries were established, in an area whose activities in ballad narrative take place largely between Berwick and Alnwick in the east, and Carlisle and Dumfries in the west. This constitutes the Borders, its people knowing themselves as Borderers first, Scots or English second, and owing their first allegiance to kin and laird rather than to Edinburgh or London. It is for this reason that family

15

# The Borders

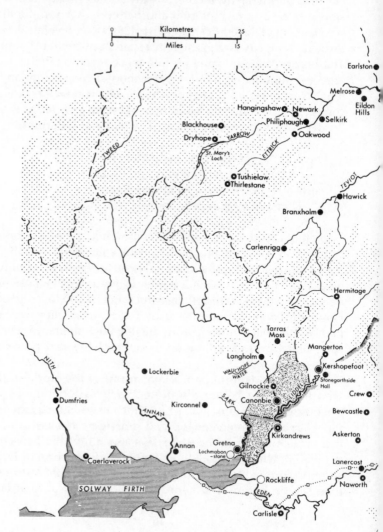

CASTLE OR TOWER     ⊙
WARDENS' MEETING PLACE     ○
SITE OF BATTLE     ⚔ 1513

DEBATABLE LAND

Boundaries
NATIONAL
MARCH

LAND OVER 1000 FT.

Kilometres 0 — 25
Miles 0 — 15

Earlston

Melrose

Eildon Hills

Hangingshaw   Newark

Blackhouse
Dryhope   YARROW
St. Mary's Loch

Philiphaugh   Selkirk
Oakwood

TWEED

ETTRICK

Tushielaw
Thirlestane

TEVIOT

Hawick

Branxholm

Carlenrigg

Hermitage

Tarras Moss

Mangerton
Kershopefoot
Stonegarthside Hall

ESK

Langholm
WAUCHOPE WATER

LIDDEL

Crew

Lockerbie

Gilnockie
Canonbie

Bewcastle

NITH

Dumfries

ANNAN

Kirconnel

SARK

Kirkandrews

Askerton

Lanercost

Annan
Gretna
Lochmabon-stone

Caerlaverock

SOLWAY FIRTH

Rockliffe

EDEN

Naworth

Carlisle

names are so vital to an understanding of the literature and history of the region, often linked in a defining manner to places, since so many of the surnames were the same. Jock o' the Side, for example, belonged to the notorious Armstrong family, distinguished from its other members by his place of residence, the tower of Syid near Mangerton in Liddesdale. Jamie Telfer of the Fair Dodhead takes his title from a Teviotdale pele. This conjunction was often abridged and characters named simply by their dwelling or, collectively, by the river on whose banks they lived. When Jamie Telfer, raided by the English, appeals for help to his protector, Buccleuch of Branksome, the laird replies:

'Gar warn the water, braid and wide,
    Gar warn it sune and hastilie!
They that winna ride for Telfer's kye
    Let them never look in the face o' me!

'Warn Wat o' Harden and his sons,
    Wi' them will Borthwick Water ride;
Warn Gaudilands and Allanhaugh,
    And Gilmanscleugh, and Commonside.'

Such ringing lines exemplify the vital and complex structure of family relationships and the personal rather than political nature of Border foray. Few Border Ballads commemorate hostilities at a national military level; 'The Battle of Otterburn' is an outstanding exception, though even here personalities predominate. Most celebrate raid, feud and vengeance in terms of kinship and family allegiances which take precedence over nationality, so that in 'The Death of Parcy Reed' (p.94) we find an English family, the Halls of Redesdale, in league with a Scottish family, the Crosiers of Teviotdale, in the destruction of their English neighbour, Parcy Reed. Cross-border alliances were of course officially discouraged, as were more intimate associations such as football matches and marriages, but remoteness from the capitals, at least before the Union of the Crowns in 1603, meant that national demands were difficult to implement.

One measure of enforcement was the system of administration: local Wardens were appointed by their respective crowns. On either side of the accepted border-line the territory was divided into three Marches, West, Middle and East, each controlled by a Warden and his assistants backed by a fluctuating and inadequate supply of troops. Remote, underpaid and frequently forgotten, Wardens had an unenviable task in so scattered and explosive a community. Their understandable frustration ignites from time to time in communications to their distant masters in Edinburgh and London. On 12 July 1587 Sir Cuthbert Collingwood, Deputy Warden of the Middle March, writes to Lord Walsingham:

I was boulde of late to wryte unto your honour, the ruenous state of this beggerly border, evne so urged by the lamentable spectacle therof, from time to time rather agravayted then reformed, for that nowe of late, in extremitie, exseding all other times of pretended peace to my knoledge, the Scottes in hostiall and warlyke maner, have burned ransomed and utterly impovereshed a greate parte of the Myddle Marche . . . I am so prycked with the daylye vewe of the abewsed, that I cannot let slippe with sylence one my parte that which be- hoveth all good subjects to reveale. Wherein I humbly crave and intently beseche your honour (for Godes sake) to be a mean to her Majestie, that we may be protected and have some deffence . . .

Such correspondence is typical, and a fair indication of the source of such ballads as 'Jamie Telfer', 'Parcy Reed', 'Kinmont Willie' and 'Jock o' the Side'.

The areas of greatest activity were those wildest parts of the West and Middle Marches, suitable for short-range incursions through patrolled valley and by guarded ford; the more easily traversed territory of the East Marches was too exposed to surveil- lance and remains poor in ballads. The Riding Ballads, as well as the ballads of Romance and the Supernatural, spring from these central and western valleys, traced by the waters of Esk,

Liddel, Yarrow, Teviot and Tweed, and from Tynedale and Redesdale in Northumberland.

Because of their territorial relevance, the ballads reprinted here have been arranged roughly in relation to the Marches, with Supernatural, largely unlocalized themes grouped separately.

Since they are part of an oral tradition, ballad origins remain obscure, and in studying these narratives it is well to remember that the vitality of oral renderings, with variants according to the singer's nationality or family, is diminished by print. James Hogg's mother, who supplied Scott with so many verses, spoke with prophetic bitterness when she declared: 'There was never ane o' my songs prentit till ye prentit them yoursel', and ye hae spoilt them a'togither. They were made for singin' and no for readin', but ye hae broken the charm now, an' they'll never be sung mair.'

Nevertheless, the singing continued, though literary scholarship laid a heavy hand on some ballads, especially before Scott's *Minstrelsy* appeared, while the degenerate broadside style of the seventeenth century is well represented in the popular 'Chevy Chase' (1624) so admired by Addison; it marks a distinct decline from the regional vigour of Bishop Percy's great discovery, 'The Battle of Otterburn'.

For this story of the conflict between Northumbrian Percy and Scottish Douglas we have the contemporary historical account of Froissart's *Chronicles* to refer to as a control. 'Chevy Chase' and its predecessor 'The Hunting of the Cheviot' are little more than tales of a hunting skirmish, but the actuality of the battle fought in Redesdale in 1388 is sharply realized in two versions of the incident. Though their leader was killed, the invading Scots were victorious. A Scottish ballad account of the affray was assembled by Scott and Hogg from a ballad which originally appeared in David Herd's *Scottish Songs* of 1776, with which they combined ocally recited fragments and some additions of their own. The pallad reproduced here (p.107) is Percy's discovery, a British Museum manuscript generally believed to date from the early sixteenth century; it clearly presents an English, indeed a Northumbrian view of the battle.

20

Riding Ballads of the West and Middle Marches are much taken up with the exploits of the Armstrongs and the Elliots. A tract of 1590 addressed to Lord Burghley runs:

The chiefe Armstrong is of Mangerton, and the chiefe Elwood [Elliot] at Cariston. These are two great surnames and most offensive to England at this daie, for the Armestronges, both of Annerdale and Lyddelsdale be ever ryding.

The matter of these ballads is not only the description of the success or failure of an inroad; we find evoked in the compact spaciousness of their stanzas an ingeniously integrated society, a closely woven moral and social fabric, the people for the most part deprived of material comforts and estranged from the consolations of religion. Apart from the ballads, true memorials to the embattled poverty of their lives remain in the pele towers, most now ruinous, to be found scattered over field, fell, farm and vicarage throughout the Marches. These grim stone dwellings measure roughly thirty-five feet by twenty-five feet, with walls anything from four to ten feet thick, rising to three storeys. Above a tunnel-vaulted basement used for storage and cattle lay the main living-room, reached by a ladder and a trap-door which could be sealed at times of attack. Above this was another room surmounted outside by a walkway with a corner look-out turret to which a firepan was attached where an alarm beacon would be lighted when the pele was under assault. Jamie Telfer is raided by the Captain of Bewcastle:

And when they cam to the Fair Dodhead
    Right hastily they clam the peel;
They loosed the kye out, ane and a',
    And ranshackled the house right weel.

Ransacking entailed the removal of as much 'gear and insight' as the attackers could carry off or drive away: cattle and the contents of the tower. It rarely amounted to much. At the end of the

21

will of Clement Reed of Elsdon, in Redesdale, in 1582, an inventory is given of his possessions; the last entry reads: 'Item inseth gere Xs' (Item, Household goods ten shillings). At the rate of the time, the contents of the pele amounted to about half the price of a cow.

The less fortunate raiders suffered capture, like Kinmont Willie or Jock o' the Side. The latter ballad opens with a lively announcement of such an event. A counterplot and a rescue attempt develop:

> Now Liddesdale has ridden a raid,
>> But I wat they had better hae staid at hame;
> For Michael o' Winfield he is dead,
>> And Jock o' the Side is prisoner ta'en.

Jock is eventually rescued to the accompaniment of humorous asides and gibes against the authorities. But not all ballad escapades end so fortunately. Hobie Noble, outlawed but loyal to his companions ('I'll be a guide worth ony twa') is betrayed and executed in Carlisle, refusing to turn traitor himself: 'I wad betray nae lad alive / For a' the goud in Christentie.'

Border allegiance, either to kin or to the family from which black mail had been taken, was not always honoured, as we find in the story of Jamie Telfer; at its best, however, such loyalty imposed a duty not only to help those in trouble but also to seek revenge on the feuding opponent – sometimes, as in the case of 'The Raid of the Reidswire', many years after the original offence. Family feud was endemic. One correspondent, John Fern, having a request from London to explain this term, replied with succinct acerbity, 'Deadly foed, the word of enmitye in the Borders, implacable without the blood and whole family distroied'. It is the ground of 'The Death of Parcy Reed'.

However, whether they live to raid again or die on the scaffold, these men are the ballad heroes – violent, lawless, clannish and vehemently opposed to Warden and Warden's men, they are celebrated indirectly like Hobie Noble, Kinmont Willie or Jock o'

22

the Side, or lauded directly when, like Johnie Armstrong, they are destroyed by the law:

John murdered was at Carlinrigg,
 And all his gallant companie:
But Scotland's heart was never sae wae,
 To see sae mony brave men die.

Because they saved their country deir
 Frae Englishmen; nane were sae bauld
While Johnie lived on the border-side,
 Nane of them durst come neir his hald.

Two other ballad themes remain to be considered in this regional context: Romance and the Supernatural, themes frequently interwoven with tragedy, frequently located in the Yarrow valley. Romantic ballads often tell the story of forbidden love where the lovers, like Romeo and Juliet, belong to families at feud and where consequently the duties of kinship loyalty exact blood vengeance. Minstrel art, however, expresses grief with an elegance touching enough to qualify an excessive stress on bloodshed, as we find for example in 'The Dowie Dens of Yarrow' (p.124):

'Now haud your tongue, my daughter dear!
 For a' this breeds but sorrow;
I'll wed thee to a better lord
 Than him ye lost on Yarrow.'

'O haud your tongue, my father dear,
 Ye mind me but of sorrow;
A fairer rose did never bloom
 Than now lies cropp'd on Yarrow.'

Ballad laments achieve their effects quietly, unadorned by the rhetoric of literary lyricism or reflective sentimentality. The dead lovers in 'The Douglas Tragedy' are buried close together:

23

Out o' the lady's grave grew a bonny red rose,
    And out o' the knight's a brier.

And they twa met, and they twa plat
    And fain they wad be near;
And a' the world might ken right weel,
    They were twa lovers dear.

A touching picture, instantly redrawn by the concluding stanza:

But by and rade the Black Douglas,
    And wow but he was rough!
For he pull'd up the bonny brier
    And flang't in St Mary's Loch.

Tragedies of love on the medieval Borders (and ballad romance is essentially tragic) are frequently lived out on a different border, between this world and another; we catch a glimpse of the medieval mind here when we recognize that the two worlds interpenetrate, both represented with a persuasive realism bearing no trace of disingenuous gentility. When Janet in 'Tamlane' (p.153) is made pregnant by the enchanted Tam she refuses either to acknowledge the father or to be married off:

'If that I gae wi' child, father,
    Myself maun bear the blame;
There's ne'er a laird about your ha'
    Shall get the bairn's name.'

Through loyalty to her true love, Janet wins back Tam from the fairy world, though not before she has endured terrors which strongly symbolize a sexual encounter.

In 'The Broomfield Hill' (p.162), the heroine's dilemma is resolved by witchcraft, though in 'The Cruel Mother' (p.170) nothing is so easy. Ballad maidenheads may be lost or saved, but unwanted

24

motherhood provides a sad social comment in this song, a tale of infanticide told with skilful economy. The mother bears, loves, kills and buries the child whose spirit then returns to confront her:

O sweet babe and thou wert mine,
    Fine flowers in the valley,
I wad cleed thee in the silk so fine,
    And the green leaves they grow rarely.

O mother dear, when I was thine,
    Fine flowers in the valley,
You didna prove to me sae kind,
    And the green leaves they grow rarely.

However corrupted by later hands and literary manners, these Border songs are a key to understanding those who created them: men and women whose lives are rarely evidenced in any other way; inhabitants of a harsh, remote and impoverished country devising their own identity as Borderers and singing their own history with its brutality, bloodshed and vengeance with humour, vigour, insight and tenderness and, in the best of them, an enviable, natural grace.

*A note on the text*

The ballads in this volume are taken from Sir Walter Scott's *Minstrelsy of the Scottish Border*, and F.J. Child's *English and Scottish Popular Ballads*. I have made minor alterations in the interests of consistency and clarity without, I hope, obscuring the characteristics of period and place.

# Suggestions for Further Study

## (a) Books:

Alan Bold, *The Ballad* (Methuen, 1979).

B.H. Bronson, *The Traditional Tunes of the Child Ballads*, 4 vols. (Princeton, 1959-72).

F.J. Child, *The English and Scottish Popular Ballads*, 4 vols. (1882-98; reprinted, Dover, 1965).

G.M. Fraser, *The Steel Bonnets* (Barrie and Jenkins, 1971).

M.J.C. Hodgart, *The Ballads* (Hutchinson, 1950).

James Reed, *The Border Ballads* (Athlone, 1973).

Sir Walter Scott, *Minstrelsy of the Scottish Border*, ed. T. Henderson (Harrap, 1931).

Godfrey Watson, *The Border Reivers* (Robert Hale, 1974).

## (b) Records:

*The Child Ballads* I & II (Topic 12T 160, 161).

*The Muckle Sangs* (Tangent TNGM119D).

A.L. Lloyd & Ewan MacColl, *English and Scottish Folk Ballads* (Topic 12T103).

Willie Scott, *The Shepherd's Song* (Topic 12T183).

Peggy Seeger & Ewan MacColl, *The Long Harvest* (Decca DA 66-75).

BALLADS OF THE WEST MARCHES

# KINMONT WILLIE
## [Child 186]

This incident took place on 13 April 1596. The hero was William
Armstrong, called Will of Kinmonth, of Morton Tower in the
Debatable Land.

Salkeld was deputy to Lord Scroope, Lord Warden of the English
West March; he is 'false' because he has broken Border Law in
taking Kinmont during the twenty-four-hour truce which followed
a Warden's meeting.

Hairibee: the place of execution in Carlisle.

Bateable Land: the Debatable Land. Barren territory of disputed
nationality around the junction of the Rivers Esk and Liddell,
notorious for its shifting population of outlaws.


O have ye na heard o' the fause Sakelde?
    O have ye na heard o' the keen Lord Scroope?
How they hae ta'en bauld Kinmont Willie,
    On Hairibee to hang him up?

Had Willie had but twenty men,
    But twenty men as stout as he,
Fause Sakelde had never the Kinmont ta'en
    Wi' eight score in his companie.

They band his legs beneath the steed,
    They tied his hands behind his back;
They guarded him fivesome on each side,
    And they brought him ower the Liddel-rack.

They led him thro' the Liddel-rack
    And also thro' the Carlisle sands;
They brought him to Carlisle castell
    To be at my Lord Scroope's commands.

'My hands are tied but my tongue is free,
    And wha will dare this deed avow?
Or answer by the border law?
    Or answer to the bauld Buccleuch?'

'Now haud thy tongue, thou rank reiver!
    There's never a Scot shall set thee free;
Before ye cross my castle-yate
    I trow ye shall take farewell o' me.'

'Fear na ye that, my lord,' quo' Willie;
    'By the faith o' my body, Lord Scroope,' he said,
'I never yet lodged in a hostelrie
    But I paid my lawing before I gaed.'

Now word is gane to the bauld Keeper
    In Branksome Ha' where that he lay,
That Lord Scroope has ta'en the Kinmont Willie,
    Between the hours of night and day.

He has ta'en the table wi' his hand,
    He garr'd the red wine spring on hie;
'Now Christ's curse on my head,' he said,
    'But avenged of Lord Scroope I'll be!

'O is my basnet a widow's curch?
    Or my lance a wand of the willow-tree?
Or my arm a lady's lily hand?
    That an English lord should lightly me!

'And have they ta'en him, Kinmont Willie,
    Against the truce of Border tide?
And forgotten that the bauld Buccleuch
    Is Keeper here on the Scottish side?

'And have they e'en ta'en him, Kinmont Willie,
    Withouten either dread or fear?
And forgotten that the bauld Buccleuch
    Can back a steed, or shake a spear?

'O were there war between the lands,
    As well I wot that there is none,
I would slight Carlisle castle high,
    Tho' it were builded of marble stone.

'I would set that castle in a low,
    And sloken it with English blood!
There's never a man in Cumberland,
    Should ken where Carlisle castle stood.

'But since nae war's between the lands,
    And there is peace, and peace should be;
I'll neither harm English lad or lass,
    And yet the Kinmont freed shall be!' –

He has called him forty marchmen bauld,
    I trow they were of his ain name,
Except Sir Gilbert Elliot call'd,
    The Laird of Stobs, I mean the same.

He has called him forty marchmen bauld,
    Were kinsmen to the bauld Buccleuch
With spur on heel, and splent on spauld,
    And gleuves of green, and feathers blue.

There were five and five before them a'
    Wi' hunting horns and bugles bright;
And five and five came wi' Buccleuch,
    Like warden's men, array'd for fight:

And five and five, like mason gang,
    That carried the ladders lang and hie;
And five and five like broken men;
    And so they reach'd the Woodhouselee.

And as we cross'd the Bateable Land,
    When to the English side we held,
The first o' men that we met wi',
    Whae sould it be but fause Sakelde?

'Where be ye gaun, ye hunters keen?'
    Quo' fause Sakelde; 'come tell to me!'
'We go to hunt an English stag,
    Has trespassed on the Scots countrie.'

'Where be ye gaun, ye marshal men?'
    Quo fause Sakelde; 'come tell me true!'
'We go to catch a rank reiver,
    Has broken faith wi' the bauld Buccleuch.'

'Where are ye gaun ye mason lads,
    Wi' a' your ladders, lang and hie?'
'We gang to herry a corbie's nest,
    That wons not far frae Woodhouselee.'

'Where be ye gaun, ye broken men?'
    Quo' fause Sakelde; 'come tell to me!'
Now Dickie of Dryhope led that band,
    And the never a word o' lear had he.

'Why trespass ye on the English side,
    Row-footed outlaws, stand!' quo' he;
The never a word had Dickie to say,
    Sae he thrust the lance through his fause body.

Then on we held for Carlisle town,
   And at Staneshaw-bank the Eden we cross'd;
The water was great and meikle of spate,
   But the never a horse nor man we lost.

And when we reached the Staneshaw-bank,
   The wind was rising loud and hie;
And there the laird garr'd leave our steeds,
   For fear that they should stamp and nie.

And when we left the Staneshaw-bank,
   The wind began full loud to blaw;
But 'twas wind and weet, and fire and sleet,
   When we came beneath the castle wa'.

We crept on knees, and held our breath,
   Till we placed the ladders against the wa';
And sae ready was Buccleuch himsell
   To mount the first before us a'.

He has ta'en the watchman by the throat,
   He flung him down upon the lead –
'Had there not been peace between our land,
   Upon the other side thou hadst gaed! –

'Now sound out trumpets!' quo' Buccleuch;
   'Let's waken Lord Scroope right merrily!'
Then loud the warden's trumpet blew –
   *'O wha dare meddle wi' me?'*

Then speedily to work we gaed,
   And raised the slogan ane and a',
And cut a hole through a sheet of lead,
   And so we won to the castle ha'.

They thought King James and a' his men
    Had won the house wi' bow and spear;
It was but twenty Scots and ten,
    That put a thousand in sic a stear!

Wi' coulters and wi' fore-hammers,
    We garred the bars bang merrily,
Until we cam to the inner prison,
    Where Willie o' Kinmont he did lie.

And when we cam to the lower prison,
    Where Willie o' Kinmont he did lie –
'O sleep ye, wake ye, Kinmont Willie,
    Upon the morn that thou's to die?'

'O I sleep saft, and I wake aft;
    It's lang since sleeping was fleyed frae me!
Gie my service back to my wife and bairns,
    And a' gude fellows that speer for me.'

Then Red Rowan has hente him up,
    The starkest man in Teviotdale –
'Abide, abide now Red Rowan,
    Till of my Lord Scroope I take farewell.

'Farewell, farewell, my gude Lord Scroope!
    My gude Lord Scroope, farewell!' he cried –
'I'll pay you for my lodging maill,
    When first we meet on the Border side.'

Then shoulder high, with shout and cry,
    We bore him down the ladder lang;
At every stride Red Rowan made,
    I wot the Kinmont's airns played clang!

'O mony a time,' quo' Kinmont Willie,
    'I have ridden a horse baith wild and wood;
But a rougher beast than Red Rowan,
    I ween my legs have ne'er bestrode.

'And many a time,' quo' Kinmont Willie,
    'I've pricked a horse out o'er the furze;
But since the day I backed a steed,
    I never wore sic cumbrous spurs!'

We scarce had won the Staneshaw-bank,
    When a' the Carlisle bells were rung,
And a thousand men, in horse and foot,
    Cam wi' the keen Lord Scroope along.

Buccleuch has turned to Eden water,
    Even where it flowed frae bank to brim,
And he has plunged in wi' a' his band,
    And safely swam them thro' the stream.

He turned him on the other side,
    And at Lord Scroope his glove flung he –
'If ye like na my visit in merry England,
    In fair Scotland come visit me!'

All sore astonished stood Lord Scroope,
    He stood as still as rock of stane;
He scarcely dared to trew his eyes,
    When thro' the water they had gane.

'He is either himself a devil frae hell,
    Or else his mother a witch maun be;
I wadna have ridden that wan water,
    For a' the gowd in Christentie.'

# JOCK O' THE SIDE
## [Child 187B]

The hero of this ballad, another Armstrong, is identified by his tower near Mangerton.
Ne'er played paw: never stirred.


'Now Liddisdale has ridden a raid,
    But I wat they had better staid at hame;
For Mitchel o' Winfield he is dead,
    And my son Johnie is pris'ner tane.'

For Mangerton House auld Downie is gane;
    Her coats she has kilted up to her knee,
And down the water wi' speed she rins,
    While tears in spaits fa' fast frae her ee.

Then up and bespake the Lord Mangerton:
    'What news, what news, sister Downie, to me?'
'Bad news, bad news, my Lord Mangerton;
    Mitchel is killed, and tane they hae my son Johnie.'

'Ne'er fear, sister Downie,' quo' Mangerton;
    'I hae yokes of oxen four and twentie,
My barns, my byres, and my faulds a' weel filled,
    And I'll part wi' them a' ere Johnie shall die.

'Three men I'll take to set him free,
    Weel harnessed a' wi' best o' steel;
The English rogues may hear, and drie
    The weight o' their brade swords to feel.

'The Laird's Jock ane, the Laird's Wat twa,
        Oh, Hobie Noble, thou ane maun be;
Thy coat is blue, thou hast been true,
        Since England banished thee, to me.'

Now Hobie was an English man,
        In Bewcastle-dale was bred and born;
But his misdeeds they were sae great,
        They banished him ne'er to return.

Lord Mangerton them orders gave,
        'Your horses the wrang way maun a' be shod;
Like gentlemen ye must not seem,
        But look like corn-caugers gawn ae road.

'Your armour gude ye maunna shaw,
        Nor aince appear like men o' weir;
As country lads be all arrayed,
        Wi' branks and brecham on ilk mare.'

Sae now a' their horses are shod the wrang way,
        And Hobie has mounted his gray sae fine,
Jock his lively bay, Wat's on his white horse behind,
        And on they rode for the water o' Tyne.

At the Cholerford they a' light down,
        And there, wi' the help o' the light o' the moon,
A tree they cut, wi' fifteen naggs upo' ilk side,
        To climb up the wa' o' Newcastle town.

But when they cam to Newcastle town
        And were alighted at the wa',
They fand their tree three ells o'er laigh,
        They fand their stick baith short and sma'.

Then up and spake the Laird's ain Jock,
    There's naething for't, the gates we maun force;'
But when they cam the gates unto,
    A proud porter withstood baith men and horse.

His neck in twa I wat they hae wrung,
    Wi' hand or foot he ne'er played paw;
His life and his keys at anes they hae tane,
    And cast his body ahind the wa'.

Now soon they reach Newcastle jail,
    And to the pris'ner thus they call:
'Sleips thou, wakes thou, Jock o' the Side?
    Or is thou wearied o' thy thrall?'

Jock answers thus, wi' dolefu' tone:
    Aft, aft I wake, I seldom sleip;
But wha's this kens my name sae weel,
    And thus to hear my waes does seek?

Then up and spake the good Laird's Jock,
    'Ne'er fear ye now, my billie,' quo' he;
'For here's the Laird's Jock, the Laird's Wat,
    And Hobie Noble come to set thee free.'

'Oh, had thy tongue, and speak nae mair,
    And o' thy tawk now let me be!
For if a' Liddisdale were here the night,
    The morn's the day that I maun die.

'Full fifteen stane o' Spanish iron
    They hae laid a' right sair on me;
Wi' locks and keys I am fast bound
    Into this dungeon mirk and drearie.'

'Fear ye no that,' quo' the Laird's Jock;
 'A faint heart ne'er wan a fair ladie;
Work thou within, we'll work without,
 And I'll be bound we set thee free.'

The first strong door that they cam at,
 They loosed it without a key;
The next chained door that they cam at,
 They gar'd it a' in flinders flee.

The pris'ner now upo' his back,
 The Laird's Jock's gotten up fu' hie;
And down the stair him, irons and a',
 Wi nae sma' speed and joy brings he.

'Now, Jock, I wat,' quo' Hobie Noble,
 Part o' the weight ye may lay on me;'
'I wat weel no,' quo' the Laird's Jock,
 'I count him lighter than a flee.'

Sae out at the gates they a' are gane,
 The pris'ner's set on horseback hie;
And now wi' speed they've tane the gate,
 While ilk ane jokes fu' wantonlie.

'O Jock, sae winsomely 's ye ride,
 Wi' baith your feet upo' ae side!
Sae weel's ye're harnessed and sae trig!
 In troth ye sit like ony bride.'

The night, tho wat, they didna mind,
 But hied them on fu' mirrilie,
Until they cam to Cholerford brae,
 Where the water ran like mountains hie.

But when they cam to Cholerford,
    There they met with an auld man;
Says, 'Honest man, will the water ride?
    Tell us in haste, if that ye can.'

'I wat weel no,' quo' the good auld man;
    'Here I hae lived this threty yeirs and three,
And ne'er yet saw the Tyne sae big,
    Nor rinning ance sae like a sea.'

Then up and spake the Laird's saft Wat,
    The greatest coward in the company;
'Now halt, now halt, we needna try't;
    The day is come we a' maun die!'

'Poor faint-hearted thief!' quo' the Laird's Jock,
    There'll nae man die but he that's fie;
I'll lead ye a' right safely through;
    Lift ye the pris'ner on ahint me.'

Sae now the water they a' hae tane,
    By anes and twas they a' swam through;
'Here we are a' safe,' says the Laird's Jock,
    'And, poor faint Wat, what think ye now?'

They scarce the ither side had won,
    When twenty men they saw pursue;
Frae Newcastle town they had been sent,
    A' English lads, right good and true.

But when the land-sergeant the water saw,
    'It winna ride, my lads,' quo' he;
Then out he cries, 'Ye the pris'ner may take,
    But leave the irons, I pray, to me.'

'I wat weel no,' cried the Laird's Jock,
    'I'll keep them a', shoon to my mare they'll be;
My good grey mare, for I am sure,
    She's bought them a' fu' dear frae thee.'

Sae now they're away for Liddesdale,
    E'en as fast as they could them hie;
The pris'ner's brought to his ain fire-side,
    And there o 's irons they make him free.

'Now, Jock, my billie,' quo' a' the three,
    'The day was comed thou was to die;
But thou's as weel at thy ain fire-side,
    Now sitting, I think, tween thee and me.'

They hae gar'd fill up ae punch-bowl,
    And after it they maun hae anither,
And thus the night they a' hae spent,
    Just as they had been brither and brither.

# HOBIE NOBLE
*[Child 189]*

Hobie is a diminutive of Halbert. The action centres on Bewcastle
Waste, a stretch of fell between Liddesdale and N. Tynedale.
   Keep good ray: keep close to me.
   At little ee: little in awe.


Foul fa' the breast first treason bred in!
    That Liddesdale may safely say:
For in it there was baith meat and drink,
    And corn unto our geldings gay.

We were stout-hearted men and true,
    As England it did often say;
But now we may turn our backs and fly,
    Since brave Noble is seld away.

Now Hobie he was an English man,
    And born into Bewcastle dale,
But his misdeeds they were sae great,
    They banished him to Liddesdale.

At Kershope-foot the tryst was set,
    Kershope of the lily lee;
And there was traitor Sim o' the Mains,
    With him a private companie.

Then Hobie has graithed his body weel,
    I wat it was wi' baith good iron and steel;
And he has pulled out his fringed grey,
    And there, brave Noble, he rade him weel.

Then Hobie is down the water gane,
    E'en as fast as he may drie;
Tho' they should a' brusten and broken their hearts,
    Frae that tryst Noble he would not be.

'Well may ye be, my feiries five!
    And aye, what is your wills wi' me?'
Then they cryed a' wi' ae consent,
    Thou'rt welcome here, brave Noble, to me.

Wilt thou with us in England ride?
    And thy safe-warrand we will be,
If we get a horse worth a hundred punds
    Upon his back that thou shalt be.

'I dare not with you into England ride,
    The land-sergeant has me at feid;
I know not what evil may betide
    For Peter of Whitfield his brother's dead.

'And Anton Shiel, he loves not me,
    For I gat twa drifts of his sheep;
The great Earl of Whitfield loves me not,
    For nae gear frae me he e'er could keep.

'But will ye stay till the day gae down,
    Until the night come o'er the grund,
And I'll be a guide worth ony twa
    That may in Liddesdale be fund.

Tho' dark the night as pick and tar,
    I'll guide ye o'er yon hills fu' hie,
And bring ye a' in safety back,
    If you'll be true and follow me.'

He's guided them o'er moss and muir,
    O'er hill and houp, and mony ae down,
Till they came to the Foulbogshiel,
    And there brave Noble he lighted down.

Then word is gane to the land-sergeant,
    At Askerton where that he lay:
'The deer that ye hae hunted lang
    Is seen into the Waste this day.'

'Then Hobie Noble is that deer:
    I wat he carries the style fu' hie!
Aft has he beat your slough-hounds back,
    And set yourselves at little ee.

'Gar warn the bows of Hartlie-burn,
    See they shaft their arrows on the wa'!
Warn Willeva and Spear Edom,
    And see the morn they meet me a'.

'Gar meet me on the Rodrie-haugh,
    And see it be by break o' day;
And we will on to Conscouthart Green,
    For there, I think, we'll get our prey.'

Then Hobie Noble has dreamed a dream,
    In the Foulbogshiel where that he lay;
He thought his horse was 'neath him shot,
    And he himself got hard away.

The cocks could crow, and the day could dawn,
    And I wat so even fell down the rain;
If Hobie had no wakened at that time,
    In the Foulbogshiel he had been ta'en or slain.

'Get up, get up, my feiries five –
    For I wat here makes a fu' ill day –
And the warst clock of this companie
    I hope shall cross the Waste this day.'

Now Hobie thought the gates were clear,
    But, ever alas! it was not sae;
They were beset wi' cruel men and keen,
    That away brave Noble could not gae.

'Yet follow me, my feiries five,
    And see of me ye keep good ray,
And the worst clock of this companie
    I hope shall cross the Waste this day.'

There was heaps of men now Hobie before,
    And other heaps was him behind,
That had he been as wight as Wallace was
    Away brave Noble he could not win.

Then Hobie had but a laddie's sword,
    But he did more than a laddie's deed;
In the midst of Conscouthart Green,
    He brake it o'er Jers a Wigham's head.

Now they have ta'en brave Hobie Noble,
    Wi' his ain bowstring they band him sae;
And I wat his heart was ne'er sae sair
    As when his ain five band him on the brae.

They have ta'en him on for West Carlisle;
    They asked him if he knew the way;
Whate'er he thought, yet little he said;
    He knew the way as well as they.

They hae ta'en him up the Ricker-gate;
　　The wives they cast their windows wide,
And ilka wife to anither can say,
　　That's the man loosed Jock o' the Side!

'Fy on ye, women! why ca' ye me man?
　　For it's nae man that I'm used like;
I'm but like a forfoughen hound,
　　Has been fighting in a dirty syke.'

Then they hae ta'en him up thro' Carlisle town,
　　And set him by the chimney-fire;
They gave brave Noble a wheat loaf to eat,
　　And that was little his desire.

Then they gave him a wheat loaf to eat
　　And after that a can o' beer;
Then they cried a', wi' ae consent,
　　Eat, brave Noble, and make good cheer!

Confess my lord's horse, Hobie, they say,
　　And the morn in Carlisle thou 's no die;
'How shall I confess them?' Hobie says,
　　'For I never saw them with mine eye.'

Then Hobie has sworn a fu' great aith,
　　By the day that he was gotten or born,
He never had onything o' my lord's
　　That either eat him grass or corn.

'Now fare thee weel, sweet Mangerton!
　　For I think again I'll ne'er thee see;
I wad betray nae lad alive,
　　For a' the goud in Christentie.

'And fare thee weel now, Liddesdale,
    Baith the hie land and the law!
Keep ye weel frae traitor Mains!
    For goud and gear he'll sell ye a'.

'I'd rather be ca'd Hobie Noble,
    In Carlisle whére he suffers for his faut,
Before I were ca'd traitor Mains,
    That eats and drinks of meal and maut.'

# DICK O' THE COW
## [Child 185]

'Dick of the Cow, that mad demi-lance northern borderer, who plaied his prizes with the lord Jockey so bravely' – Thomas Nashe, 1596.

To tie with St Mary knot: to hamstring.


Now Liddesdale has lain long in
    There is no riding there at a';
Their horse is growing so lidder and fat
    That are lazy in the sta'.

Then Johnie Armstrang to Willie can say,
    Billie, a riding then will we;
England and us has been long at a feud;
    Perhaps we may hit of some bootie.

Then they're com'd on to Hutton Hall,
    They rade that proper place about;
But the laird he was the wiser man,
    For he had left nae gear without.

Then he had left nae gear to steal,
    Except six sheep upon a lee;
Says Johnie, I'd rather in England die
    Before their six sheep go to Liddesdale with me.

'But how called they the man we last with met,
    Billie, as we came over the knowe?'
'That same he is an innocent fool,
    And some men calls him Dick o' the Cow.'

'That fool has three good kine of his own
    As is in a' Cumberland, billie,' quoth he:
'Betide my life, betide my death,
    These three kine shall go to Liddesdale with me.'

Then they're comed on to the poor fool's house,
    And they have broken his walls so wide;
They have loosed out Dick o' the Cow's kine three,
    And ta'en three coverlets off his wife's bed.

Then on the morn, when the day grew light,
    The shouts and cries rose loud and high:
'Hold thy tongue, my wife,' he says,
    'And of thy crying let me be.

'Hold thy tongue, my wife,' he says,
    'And of thy crying let me be,
And ay that where thou wants a cow,
    Good sooth that I shall bring thee three.'

Then Dick's comed on to lord and master,
    And I wat a dreirie fool was he:
'Hold thy tongue, my fool,' he says,
    'For I may not stand to jest with thee.'

'Shame speed a' your jesting, my lord,' quo' Dickie,
    'For nae such jesting 'grees with me;
Liddesdale has been in my house this last night,
    And they have ta'en my three kine from me.

'But I may nae langer in Cumberland dwell,
    To be your poor fool and your leal,
Unless ye give me leave, my lord,
    To go to Liddesdale and steal.'

'To give thee leave, my fool,' he says,
    'Thou speakst against mine honour and me;
Unless thou give me thy troth and thy right hand
    Thou'lt steal frae nane but them that sta' from thee.'

'There is my troth and my right hand;
    My head shall hing on Hairibee,
I'll never cross Carlisle sands again,
    If I steal frae ae man but them that's sta' frae me.'

Dickie has ta'en leave at lord and master,
    And I wot a merry fool was he;
He has bought a bridle and a pair of new spurs,
    And has packed them up in his breek-thigh.

Then Dickie's come on for Puddingburn,
    Even as fast as he may drie;
Dickie's come on for Puddingburn,
    Where there was thirty Armstrongs and three.

'What's this comed on me!' quo' Dickie,
    'What mickle wae's this happened on me,' quo' he,
'Where here is but ae innocent fool,
    And there is thirty Armstrongs and three!'

Yet he's comed up to the hall among them all;
    So well he became his courtesie:
'Well may ye be, my good Laird's Jock!
    But the de'il bless all your companie.

'I'm come to plain of your man Fair Johnie Armstrong,
    And syne his billie Willie,' quo' he;
'How they have been in my house this last night,
    And they have ta'en my three kye frae me.'

Quo' Johnie Armstrong, 'We'll him hang;'
  'Nae,' then quo' Willie, 'we'll him slay;'
But up bespake another young man, 'We'll knit him in a four-
      nooked sheet,
  Give him his burden of batts, and let him gae.'

Then up bespake the good Laird's Jock,
  The best fellow in the companie:
'Sit thy way down a little while, Dickie
  And a piece of thine own cow's hough I'll give to thee.'

But Dickie's heart it grew so great
  That never a bit of it he dought to eat;
But Dickie was 'ware of ane auld peat-house,
  Where there all night he thought for to sleep.

Then Dickie was 'ware of that auld peat-house,
  Where there all the night he thought for to lie;
And a' the prayers the poor fool prayed was,
  'I wish I had amends for my own three kye!'

Then it was the use of Puddingburn,
  And the house of Mangerton, all hail!
Those that came not at the first call
  They got no more meat till the next meal.

The lads, that hungry and aevery was,
  Above the door-head they flang the key;
Dickie took good notice to that;
  Says, 'There's bootie yonder for me.'

Then Dickie's gane into the stable,
  Where there stood thirty horse and three;
He has tied them a' with St Mary knot,
  All these horse but barely three.

He has tied them a' with St Mary knot,
    All these horse but barely three;
He has loupen on one, ta'en another in his hand,
    And out at the door and gane is Dickie.

Then on the morn, when the day grew light,
    The shouts and cries rose loud and high;
'What's that thief?' quo' the good Laird's Jock;
    'Tell me the truth and the verity.

'What's that thief?' quo' the good Laird's Jock;
    'See unto me ye do not lie.'
'Dick o' the Cow has been in the stable this last night,
    And has my brother's horse and mine frae me.'

'Ye wad never be telled it,' quo' the Laird's Jock;
    'Have ye not found my tales fu' leal?
Ye wad never out of England bide,
    Till crooked and blind and a' wad steal.'

'But will thou lend me thy bay?' Fair Johnie Armstrong can say,
    'There's nae mae horse loose in the stable but he;
And I'll either bring ye Dick o' the Cow again,
    Or the day is come when he must die.'

'To lend thee my bay,' the Laird's Jock can say,
    'He's both worth gold and good monie;
Dick o' the Cow has away twa horse,
    I wish no thou should no make him three.'

He has ta'en the Laird's jack on his back,
    The twa-handed sword that hung low by his thigh;
He has ta'en the steel cap on his head,
    And on is he to follow Dickie.

Then Dickie was not a mile off the town,
    I wat a mile but barely three,
Till John Armstrong has o'erta'en Dick o' the Cow,
    Hand for hand on Cannobie lee.

'Abide thee, bide now Dickie then,
    The day is come that thou must die;'
Dickie looked o'er his left shoulder;
    'Johnie, has thou any more in thy company?

'There is a preacher on our chapel,
    And a' the lee-lang day teaches he;
When day is gane and night is come,
    There's never a word I mark but three.

'The first and second's Faith and Conscience;
    The third is, Johnie, Take head of thee;
But what faith and conscience had thou, traitor,
    When thou took my three kye frae me?

'And when thou had ta'en my three kye,
    Thou thought in thy heart thou was no well sped;
But thou sent thy billie Willie o'er the knowe,
    And he took three co'erlets off my wife's bed.'

Then Johnie let a spear fa' low by his thigh,
    Thought well to run the innocent through;
But the powers above was more than his,
    He ran but the poor fool's jerkin through.

Together they ran or ever they blan –
    This was Dickie, the fool, and he –
Dickie could not win to him with the blade of the sword,
    But he felled him with the plummet under the eye.

Now Dickie has felled fair Johnie Armstrong,
    The prettiest man in the south country;
'Gramercy,' then can Dickie say,
    'I had twa horse, thou hast made me three.'

He has ta'en the laird's jack off his back,
    The twa-handed sword that hung low by his thigh;
He has ta'en the steel cap off his head:
    'Johnie, I'll tell my master I met with thee.'

When Johnie wakened out of his dream,
    I wat a dreary man was he:
'Is thou gane now Dickie, then?
    The shame go in thy company!

'Is thou gane now, Dickie, then?
    The shame go in thy company!
For if I should live this hundred year,
    I shall never fight with a fool after thee.'

Then Dickie comed home to lord and master,
    Even as fast as he may drie:
'Now Dickie, I shall neither eat meat nor drink
    Till high hanged that thou shalt be!'

'The shame speed the liars, my lord!' quo' Dickie,
    'That was no the promise ye made to me;
For I'd never gane to Liddesdale to steal
    Till that I sought my leave at thee.'

'But what gart thou steal the Laird's Jock's horse?
    And, limmer, what gart thou steal him?' quo' he;
'For lang might thou in Cumberland dwelt
    Or the Laird's Jock had stol'n ought frae thee.'

'Indeed I wat ye leed, my lord,
   And even so loud as I hear ye lie;
I wan him frae his man, fair Johnie Armstrong,
   Hand for hand on Cannobie lee.

'There's the jack was on his back,
   The twa-handed sword that hung low by his thigh;
There's the steel cap was on his head;
   I have a' these tokens to let you see.'

'If that be true thou to me tells –
   I trow thou dare not tell a lie –
I'll give thee twenty pound for the good horse,
   Well telled in thy cloak-lap shall be.

'And I'll give thee one of my best milk-kye,
   To maintain thy wife and children three;
And that may be as good, I think,
   As ony twa o' thine might be.'

'The shame speed the liars, my lord!' quo' Dick,
   'Trow ye ay to make a fool of me?
I'll either have thirty pound for the good horse,
   Or else he's gae to Mattan fair wi' me.'

Then he has given him thirty pound for the good horse,
   All in gold and good money;
He has given him one of his best milk-kye,
   To maintain his wife and children three.

Then Dickie's come down through Carlisle town,
   Even as fast as he may drie:
The first of men that he with met
   Was my lord's brother, Bailiff Glozenberrie.

'Well may ye be, my good Ralph Scroope!'
    'Welcome, my brother's fool!' quo' he;
'Where did thou get fair Johnie Armstrong's horse?'
    'Where did I get him but steal him,' quo' he.

'But will thou sell me fair Johnie Armstrong's horse?
    And, billie, will thou sell him to me?' quo' he:
'Ay, and tell me the money on my cloak-lap,
    For there's not one farthing I'll trust thee.'

'I'll give thee fifteen pound for the good horse,
    Well telled on thy cloak-lap shall be;
And I'll give thee one of my best milk-kye,
    To maintain thy wife and thy children three.'

'The shame speed the liars, my lord!' quo' Dickie,
    'Trow ye ay to make a fool of me?' quo' he:
'I'll either have thirty pound for the good horse,
    Or else he's to Mattan fair wi' me.'

He has given him thirty pound for the good horse,
    All in gold and good money;
He has given him one of his best milk-kye,
    To maintain his wife and children three.

Then Dickie lap a loup on high,
    And I wat a loud laughter leugh he:
'I wish the neck of the third horse were broken,
    For I have a better of my own, and any better can be.'

Then Dickie comed hame to his wife again;
    Judge ye how the poor fool he sped;
He has given her three score of English pounds
    For three auld co'erlets was ta'en off her bed.

'Hae, take thee there twa as good kye,
    I trow, as all thy three might be;
And yet here is a white-footed nag;
    I think he'll carry both thee and me.

'But I may no longer in Cumberland dwell;
    The Armstrongs, they'll hang me high:'
But Dickie has ta'en leave at lord and master,
    And Burgh under Stanemuir there dwells Dickie.

## JOHNIE ARMSTRONG
*[Child 169C]*

John Armstrong was brother to Thomas Armstrong, Laird of Mangerton (see 'Dick o' the Cow'), and lived in the tower of Gilnockie, near Langholm. The incident occurred in 1530.
    The King: James V (1512-42).


Some speaks of lords, some speaks of lairds,
    And sic like men of high degree;
Of a gentleman I sing a sang,
    Sometime called Laird of Gilnockie.

The king he writes a loving letter,
    With his ain hand sae tenderly:
And he hath sent it to Johny Armstrang,
    To come and speak with him speedily.

The Elliots and Armstrangs did convene,
    They were a gallant company:
'We'll ride and meet our lawful king,
    And bring him safe to Gilnockie.

'Make kinnen and capon ready, then,
    And venison in great plenty;
We'll welcome hame our royal king;
    I hope he'll dine at Gilnockie!'

They ran their horse on the Langholm holm
    And brake their spears with mickle main;
The ladies lukit frae their loft windows,
    'God bring our men weel back again!'

When Johny came before the king,
    With all his men sae brave to see,
The king he movit his bonnet to him;
    He weened he was king as well as he.

'May I find grace, my sovereign liege,
    Grace for my loyal men and me?
For my name it is Johny Armstrang,
    And subject of yours, my liege,' said he.

'Away, away, thou traitor strang!
    Out of my sicht thou may'st soon be!
I grantit never a traitor's life,
    And now I'll not begin with thee.'

'Grant me my life, my liege, my king,
    And a bonny gift I will give to thee;
Full four-and-twenty milk-white steeds,
    Were a' foaled in a year to me.

'I'll gie thee all these milk-white steeds,
    That prance and nicker at a spear,
With as mickle gude English gilt
    As four of their braid backs can bear.'

'Away, away, thou traitor strang!
    Out of my sicht thou may'st soon be!
I grantit never a traitor's life,
    And now I'll not begin with thee.'

'Grant me my life, my liege, my king,
    And a bonny gift I'll gie to thee;
Good four-and-twenty ganging mills,
    That gang through a' the year to me.

'These four-and-twenty mills complete
    Shall gang for thee through all the year,
And as mickle of good red wheat
    As their hoppers dow to bear.'

'Away, away, thou traitor strang!
    Out of my sicht thou may'st soon be!
I grantit never a traitor's life,
    And now I'll not begin with thee.'

'Grant me my life, my liege, my king,
    And a great gift I'll gie to thee;
Bauld four-and-twenty sisters' sons,
    Shall for thee fight tho' all should flee.'

'Away, away, thou traitor strang!
    Out of my sicht thou may'st soon be!
I grantit never a traitor's life,
    And now I'll not begin with thee.'

'Grant me my life, my liege, my king,
    And a brave gift I'll gie to thee;
All between here and Newcastle town
    Shall pay their yearly rent to thee.'

'Away, away, thou traitor strang!
    Out of my sicht thou may'st soon be!
I grantit never a traitor's life,
    And now I'll not begin with thee.'

'Ye lied, ye lied, now, king,' he says,
    Although a king and prince ye be,
For I loved naething in all my life,
    I dare well say it, but honesty;

'But a fat horse, and a fair woman,
    Twa bonny dogs to kill a deer:
But England should have found me meal and malt,
    If I had lived this hundred year!

'She should have found me meal and malt
    And beef and mutton in all plenty;
But ne'er a Scots wife could have said
    That e'er I skaithed her a poor flie.

'To seek hot water beneath cold ice,
    Surely it is a great folly;
I have asked grace at a graceless face,
    But there is nane for my men and me.

'But had I kenned, or I came frae hame, ·
    How thou unkind wadst been to me,
I wad have kept the border-side,
    In spite of all thy force and thee.

'Wist England's king that I was ta'en,
    O gin a blithe man wad he be!
For once I slew his sister's son,
    And on his breast-bane broke a tree.'

John wore a girdle about his middle,
    Embroidered o'er with burning gold,
Bespangled with the same metal,
    Most beautiful was to behold.

There hung nine targats at Johny's hat,
    And ilk ane worth three hundred pound:
'What wants that knave that a king should have,
    But the sword of honour and the crown!

'O where got thou these targats, Johnie,
    That blink sae brawly abune thy brie?'
'I gat them in the field fechting,
    Where, cruel king, thou durst not be.

'Had I my horse, and my harness gude,
    And riding as I wont to be,
It should have been told this hundred year
    The meeting of my king and me.

'God be wi' thee, Kirsty, my brither,
    Lang live thou, Laird of Mangerton!
Lang may'st thou live on the border-side
    Or thou see thy brither ride up and down.

'And God be wi' thee, Kirsty, my son,
    Where thou sits on thy nurse's knee!
But and thou live this hundred year,
    Thy father's better thou'lt never be.

'Farewell, my bonny Gilnock-Hall,
    Where on Esk-side thou standest stout!
If I had lived but seven years mair,
    I wad have gilt thee round about.'

John murdered was at Carlinrigg,
    And all his gallant companie:
But Scotland's heart was never sae wae,
    To see sae mony brave men die.

Because they saved their country deir
    Frae Englishmen; nane were sae bauld,
While Johnie lived on the border-side,
    Nane of them durst come near his hald.

# THE FRAY OF SUPORT
## [Minstrelsy]

'Of all the Border ditties which have fallen into the Editor's hands
this is by far the most uncouth and savage. It is usually chaunted
in a sort of wild recitative, except the burden, which swells into
a long and varied howl...' – Walter Scott.

John Forster: probably refers to the Warden of the English Mid-
dle March, 1560-95.

Brock-skin bag: used as ammunition pouch.


Sleep'ry Sim of the Lamb-hill,
And snoring Jock of Suport-mill,
Ye are baith right het and fou'; –
But my wae wakens na you.
Last night I saw a sorry sight –
Nought left me, o' four-and-twenty gude ousen and kye,
My weel-ridden gelding and a white quey,
But a toom byre and a wide,
And the twelve nogs on ilka side.
    Fy lads! shout a' a' a' a' a',
    My gear's a' gane.

Well may ye ken,
Last night I was right scarce o' men:
But Toppet Hob o' the Mains had guesten'd in my house by chance;
I set him to wear the fore-door wi' the speir, while I kept the back
        door wi' the lance;
But they hae run him thro' the thick o' the thie, and broke his
        knee-pan,
And the mergh o' his shin bane has run down on his spur leather
        whang:
He's lame while he lives, and wher'er he may gang.
    Fy lads! shout a' a' a' a' a'
    My gear's a' gane.

But Peenye, my gude son, is out at the Hagbut-head,
His een glittering for anger like a fiery gleed;
Crying – 'Mak sure the nooks
Of Maky's-muir crooks;
For the wily Scot takes by nooks, hooks, and crooks,
Gin we meet a' together in a head the morn,
We'll be merry men.'
    Fy lads! shout a' a' a' a' a',
    My gear's a' gane.

There's doughty Cuddy in the Heugh-head,
Thou was aye gude at a' need:
With thy brock-skin bag at thy belt,
Ay ready to make a puir man help.
Thou maun awa' out to the Cauf-craigs
(Where aince ye lost your ain twa naigs),
And there toom thy brock-skin bag.
    Fy lads! shout a' a' a' a' a',
    My gear's a' ta'en.

Doughty Dan o' the Houlet Hirst,
Thou was aye gude at a birst:
Gude wi' a bow, and better wi' a speir,
The bauldest march-man that e'er followed gear;
Come thou here.
    Fy lads! shout a' a' a' a' a',
    My gear's a' gane.

Rise, ye carle coopers, frae making o' kirns and tubs,
In the Nicol forest woods.
Your craft has na left the value of an oak rod,
But if you had had ony fear o' God,
Last night ye had na slept sae sound,
And let my gear be ta'en.
    Fy lads! shout a' a' a' a' a',
    My gear's a' ta'en.

Ah! lads, we'll fang them a' in a net!
For I hae a' the fords o' Liddel set;
The Dunkin, and the Door-loup,
The Willie-ford, and the Water-slack,
The Black-rack, and the Trout-dub of Liddel;
There stands John Forster wi' five men at his back,
Wi' buft coat and cap of steil:
Boo! ca' at them e'en Jock;
The ford's sicker, I wat weil.
    Fy lads! shout a' a' a' a' a',
    My gear's a' ta'en.

Hoo! hoo! gar raise the Reid Souter, and Ringan's Wat,
Wi a broad elshin and a wicker;
I wat weil they'll make a ford sicker.
Sae whether be Elliots or Armstrangs,
Or rough riding Scots, or rude Johnstones,
Or whether they be frae the Tarras or Ewsdale,
They maun turn and fight, or try the deeps o' Liddel.
    Fy lads! shout a' a' a' a' a',
    My gear's a' ta'en.

'Ah! but they will play ye another jigg,
For they will out at the big rig,
And thro' at Fargy Grame's gap.'
But I hae another wile for that:
For I hae little Will, and stalwart Wat,
And lang Aicky, in the Souter moor,
Wi' his sleuth dog sits in his watch right sure;
Shou'd the dog gie a bark,
He'll be out in his sark,
And die or won.
    Fy lads! shout a' a' a' a' a',
    My gear's a' ta'en.

Ha! boys – I see a party appearing – wha's yon!
Methinks it's the captain of Bewcastle, and Jephtha's John,
Coming down by the foul steps of Catlowdie's loan:
They'll make a' sicker, come which way they will.
    Ha lads! shout a' a' a' a' a',
    My gear's a' ta'en.

Captain Musgrave, and a' his band,
And coming down by the siller-strand,
And the muckle toun-bell o' Carlisle is rung:
My gear was a' weel won,
And before it's carried o'er the Border, mony a man's gae down.
    Fy lads! shout a' a' a' a' a',
    My gear's a' gane.

# FAIR HELEN OF KIRCONNELL
## [Minstrelsy]

According to Scott, Helen Irving, daughter of the Laird of Kircon-
nell in Dumfriesshire, was courted by rival lovers. She favoured
Adam Fleming of Kirkpatrick; they met in secret, and she took the
bullet intended for Fleming by his unnamed rival.


I wish I were where Helen lies!
Night and day on me she cries;
O that I were where Helen lies,
    On fair Kirconnell Lee!

Curst be the heart that thought the thought,
And curst the hand that fired the shot,
When in my arms burd Helen dropt,
    And died to succour me!

O think na ye my heart was sair,
When my love dropt down and spak nae mair!
There did she swoon wi' meikle care,
    On fair Kirconnell Lee.

As I went down the water side,
None but my foe to be my guide,
None but my foe to be my guide,
    On fair Kirconnell Lee.

I lighted down, my sword did draw,
I hacked him in pieces sma';
I hacked him in pieces sma',
    For her sake that died for me.

O Helen fair beyond compare!
I'll make a garland of thy hair,
Shall bind my heart for evermair,
    Until the day I die.

O that I were where Helen lies!
Night and day on me she cries;
Out of my bed she bids me rise,
    Says, 'Haste, and come to me!'

O Helen fair! O Helen chaste!
If I were with thee, I were blest,
Where thou liest low, and takes thy rest,
    On fair Kirconnell Lee.

I wish my grave were growing green,
A winding sheet drawn ower my een,
And I in Helen's arms lying,
    On fair Kirconnell Lee.

I wish I were where Helen lies!
Night and day on me she cries;
And I am weary of the skies,
    For her sake that died for me.

# THE LOCHMABEN HARPER
### [Child 192A]

King Henry: Scott's version replaces this with the more probable
Lord Warden, and adds a final explanatory stanza:

> Then ay he harped, and ay he carped;
> > Sae sweet were the harpings he let them hear!
> He was paid for the foal he never lost
> > And three times over for the gude GRAY MARE!

Harp and carp: tell tales to a harp accompaniment.


Heard ye e'er of the silly blind harper,
> That long lived in Lochmaben town,
How he wad gang to fair England,
> To steal King Henry's Wanton Brown?

But first he gaed to his gude wife,
> Wi' a' the speed that he could thole;
'This wark,' quo' he, 'will never wark
> Without a mare that has a foal.'

Quo' she, 'Thou hast a gude gray mare,
> That 'll rin o'er hills baith law and hie;
Gae tak the gray mare in thy hand,
> And leave the foal at hame wi' me.

'And tak a halter in thy hose,
> And o' thy purpose dinna fail;
But wap it o'er the Wanton's nose,
> And tie her to the gray mare's tail.

'Syne ca' her out at yon back gate,
    O'er moss and muir and ilka dale;
For she'll ne'er let the Wanton bite
    Till she comes hame to her ain foal.'

So he is up to England gane,
    Even as fast as he can hie,
Till he came to King Henry's gate;
    And wha was there but King Henry?

'Come in,' quo' he, 'thou silly blind harper,
    And of thy harping let me hear;'
'O, by my sooth,' quo' the silly blind harper,
    'I'd rather hae stabling for my mare.'

The king he looks o'er his left shoulder,
    And says unto his stable-groom,
'Gae tak the silly poor harper's mare,
    And tie her side my Wanton Brown.'

And ay he harpit, and ay he carpit,
    Till a' the lords had footed the floor;
They thought the music was sae sweet,
    And they forgot the stable door.

And ay he harpit, and ay he carpit,
    Till a' the nobles were sound asleep;
Then quietly he took aff his shoon,
    And saftly down the stair did creep.

Syne to the stable door he hies,
    Wi' tread as light as light could be,
And when he opened and gaed in,
    There he fand thirty gude steeds and three.

He took the halter frae his hose,
    And of his purpose did na fail;
He slipt it o'er the Wanton's nose,
    And tied it to his gray mare's tail.

He ca'd her out at yon back gate,
    O'er moss and muir and ilka dale,
And she loot ne'er the Wanton bite,
    But held her still gaun at her tail.

The gray mare was right swift o' foot,
    And did na fail to find the way,
For she was at Lochmaben gate
    Fu' lang three hours ere it was day.

When she came to the harper's door,
    There she gave mony a nicher and sneer;
'Rise,' quo' the wife, 'thou lazy lass,
    Let in thy master and his mare.'

Then up she rose, pat on her claes,
    And lookit out through the lock-hole;
'O, by my sooth,' then quo' the lass,
    'Our mare has gotten a braw big foal!'

'Come had thy peace, thou foolish lass,
    The moon's but glancing in thy eye;
I'll wad my hail fee against a groat,
    It's bigger than e'er our foal will be.'

The neighbours too that heard the noise
    Cried to the wife to put her in;
'By my sooth,' then quo' the wife,
    'She's better than ever he rade on.'

But on the morn, at fair day light,
    When they had ended a' their cheer,
King Henry's Wanton Brown was stawn,
    And eke the poor old harper's mare.

'Allace! allace!' says the silly blind harper,
    'Allace, allace, that I came here!
In Scotland I've tint a braw cowte-foal,
    In England they've stawn my gude gray mare.'

'Come had thy tongue, thou silly blind harper,
    And of thy allacing let me be;
For thou shalt get a better mare,
    And weel paid shall thy cowte-foal be.'

# BALLADS OF THE MIDDLE MARCHES (1)

# JAMIE TELFER IN THE FAIR DODHEAD
*[Child 190 add.]*

Child includes this 'unprinted copy referred to in the *Border Minstrelsy*, in which the Elliots take the place assigned in the other version to the Scotts', and notes 'Jamie Telfer *in* the Fair Dodhead suggests, according to Scottish usage, that Telfer was a tenant simply, whereas *of* would make him proprietor' (V. 249).

Martinmas: 11 November, a prime raiding season. 'The last moneths in the yeare are theyr chiefe time of stealing,' Sir Robert Carey, Warden.

Ware my dame's calfskin: use my mother's whip.

It fell about the Martinmas,
     When steeds were fed wi' corn and hay,
The Captain of Bewcastle said to his lads,
     We'll into Tiviotdale and seek a prey.

The first ae guide that they met with
     Was high up in Hardhaugh swire,
The second guide that they met with
     Was laigh down in Borthwick water.

'What tidings, what tidings, my bonny guide?'
     'Nae tidings, nae tidings I hae to thee;
But if ye'll gae to the Fair Dodhead
     Mony a cow's calf I'll let ye see.'

When they came to the Fair Dodhead,
     Right hastily they clam the peel,
And loos'd the nolt out, ane and a',
     And ranshakled the house right weel.

Now Jamie's heart it was right sair,
 The tear ay rowing in his eye;
He pled wi' the Captain to hae his gear,
 Or else revenged he would be.

But the Captain turned himself about,
 Said, 'Man, there's naething in thy house
But an auld sword without a scabbard,
 That scarcely now would fell a mouse.'

The moon was up and the sun was down,
 'T was the gryming of a new-fa'n snaw;
Jamie Telfer has run eight miles barefoot
 Between Dodhead and Branxholm Ha'.

And when he came to Branxholm Ha'
 He shouted loud and cry'd well he,
Till up bespake them auld Buccleugh,
 'Wha's this that brings the fray to me?'

'It's I, Jamie Telfer i' the Fair Dodhead,
 And a harried man I think I be;
There's naething left i' the Fair Dodhead
 But only wife and children three.'

'Gae seek your succour frae Martin Elliot,
 For succour ye's get nane frae me;
Gae seek your succour where ye paid black-mail,
 For, man, ye never paid money to me.'

Jamie he's turned him round about,
 And ay the tear blinded his eye:
'I'se never pay mail to Scott again,
 Nor the Fair Dodhead I'll ever see.'

Now Jamie is up the water-gate,
	E'en as fast as he can drie,
Till he came to the Coultart Cleugh,
	And there he shouted and cried weel he.

Then up bespake him auld Jock Grieve,
	'Whae's this that brings the fray to me?'
'It's I, Jamie Telfer i' the Fair Dodhead,
	And a harried man I think I be.

'There's naething left i' the Fair Dodhead
	But only wife and children three,
And sax poor calves stand i' the sta',
	A' routing loud for their minnie.'

'Alack, wae's me!' quo' auld Jock Grieve,
	'Alack, alack, and wae is me!
For ye was married t' the auld sister,
	And I t'the youngest o' the three.'

Then he's ta'en out a bonny black,
	It was weel fed wi' corn and hay,
And set Jamie Telfer on his back,
	To the Catlock hill to take the fray.

When he came to the Catlock hill,
	He shouted loud and cry'd weel he;
'Whae's that, whae's that,' quo' Martin's Hab,
	'Whae's this that brings the fray to me?'

'It's I, Jamie Telfer i' the Fair Dodhead,
	And a harried man I think I be;
There's naething left i' the Fair Dodhead
	But only wife and children three.'

'Alack, wae's me!' quo Martin's Hab,
    'Alack, awae, my heart is sair!
I never came by the Fair Dodhead
    That ever I fand thy basket bare.'

Then he's ta'en out a bonny black,
    It was weel fed wi' corn and hay,
And set Jamie Telfer on his back
    To the Pricken haugh to take the fray.

When he came to the Pricken haugh,
    He shouted loud and cry'd weel he;
Up then bespake auld Martin Elliot,
    'Whae's this that brings the fray to me?'

'It's I, Jamie Telfer i' the Fair Dodhead,
    And a harried man I think I be;
There's naething left i' the Fair Dodhead
    But only wife and children three.'

'Ever alack!' can Martin say,
    'And ay my heart is sair for thee!
But fy, gar ca' on Simmy my son,
    And see that he come hastily.

'Fy, gar warn the water-side,
    Gar warn it soon and hastily;
Them that winna ride for Telfer's kye,
    Let them never look i' the face o' me.

'Gar warn the water, braid and wide,
    And warn the Currers i' the shaw;
When ye come in at the Hermitage slack,
    Warn doughty Willie o' Gorrenberry.'

The gear was driven the Frostylee up,
    From the Frostylee into the plain;
When Simmy looked him afore,
    He saw the kye right fast driving.

'Whae drives the kye,' then Simmy can say,
    'To make an outspeckle o' me?'
'It's I, the Captain o' Bewcastle, Simmy,
    I winna lain my name frae thee.'

'O will ye let the gear gae back?
    Or will ye do ony thing for me?'
'I winna let the gear gae back,
    Nor naething, Simmy, I'll do for thee.

'But I'll drive Jamie Telfer's kye
    In spite o' Jamie Telfer's teeth and thee;'
'Then by my sooth,' can Simmy say,
    'I'll ware thy dame's calfskin on thee.

'Fa' on them, lads!' can Simmy say,
    'Fy, fa' on them cruelly!
For or they win to the Ritter ford
    Mony toom saddle there shall be.'

But Simmy was stricken o'er the head,
    And thro' the knapscap it is gane,
And Moscrop made a doleful rage
    When Simmy on the ground lay slain.

'Fy, lay on them!' quo' Martin Elliot,
    'Fy, lay on them cruelly!
For ere they win to the Kershope ford
    Mony toom saddle there shall be'

John o' Biggam he was slain,
    And John o' Barlow, as I heard say,
And fifteen o' the Captain's men
    Lay bleeding on the ground that day.

The Captain was shot through the head,
    And also through the left ba' stane;
Tho' he had lived this hundred years,
    He's ne'er been lo'ed by woman again.

The word is gane unto his bride,
    E'en in the bower where she lay,
That her good lord was in's enemy's land
    Since into Tiviotdale he led the way.

'I lourd a had a winding sheet
    And helped to put it o'er his head,
Or he's been ta'en in's enemy's lands,
    Since he o'er Liddel his men did lead.'

There was a man in our company,
    And his name was Willie Wudespurs:
'There is a house in the Stanegarside,
    If any man will ride with us.'

When they came to the Stanegarside,
    They banged wi' trees and brake the door,
They loosed the kye out ane and a',
    And set them furth our lads before.

There was an auld wif ayont the fire,
    A wee bit o' the Captain's kin:
'Whae looses out the Captain's kye,
    And sae mony o' the Captain's men within?'

'I, Willie Wudespurs, let out the kye,
    I winna lain my name frae thee,
And I'll loose out the Captain's kye
    In spite o' the Captain's teeth and thee.'

Now on they came to the Fair Dodhead,
    They were a welcome sight to see,
And instead of his ain ten milk-kye
    Jamie Telfer's gotten thirty and three.

# THE OUTLAW MURRAY
*[Minstrelsy]*

The origin of this tale remains obscure.

Ettrick forest is a fair forest,
    In it grows many a seemly tree;
There's hart and hind, and dae and rae,
    And of a' wild beasts great plenty.

There's a fair castle, bigged wi' lime and stane;
    O! gin it stands not pleasantly!
In the forefront o' that castle fair,
    Twa unicorns are bra' to see;
There's the picture of a knight, and a lady bright,
    And the green hollin abune their brie.

There an outlaw keeps five hundred men;
    He keeps a royal company!
His merrymen are a' in ae livery clad,
    O' the Linkome green sae gay to see;
He and his lady in purple clad,
    O! gin they lived not royally!

Word is gane to our noble King,
    In Edinburgh where that he lay,
That there was an outlaw in Ettrick Forest,
    Counted him nought, nor a' his courtrie gay.

'I make a vow,' then the good King said,
    'Unto the man that dear bought me,
I'se either be King of Ettrick Forest,
    Or King of Scotland that outlaw sall be!'

Then spak the lord, hight Hamilton,
    And to the noble king said he,
'My sovereign prince, some counsel take,
    First at your nobles, syne at me.

'I redd ye, send yon braw outlaw till,
    And see if your man come will he:
Desire him come and be your man,
    And hald you of yon Forest free.

'If he refuses to do that,
    We'll conquess baith his lands and he!
Or else, we'll throw his castle down,
    And make a widow o' his gay lady.'

The King then called a gentleman,
    James Boyd (the Earl of Arran his brother was he),
When James he cam before the King,
    He knelt before him on his knee.

'Welcome, James Boyd!' said our noble King;
    'A message ye maun gang for me;
Ye maun hie to Ettrick Forest
    To yon outlaw, where bideth he:

'Ask him of whom he holds his lands,
    Or man, wha may his master be,
And desire him come, and be my man,
    And hold of me yon Forest free.

'To Edinburgh to come and gang,
    His safe warrant I sall gie;
And if he refuses to do that,
    We'll conquess baith his lands and he.

'Thou may's vow I'll cast his castle down,
    And mak a widow o' his gay lady;
I'll hang his merrymen, pair by pair,
    In ony frith where I may them see.'

James Boyd took his leave o' the noble King,
    To Ettrick Forest fair cam he;
Down Birkendale Brae when that he cam,
    He saw the fair Forest wi' his e'e.

Baith dae and rae, and hart and hind,
    And of a' wild beastis great plentie;
He heard the bows that bauldly ring,
    And arrows whidderan' him near by.

Of that fair castle he got a sight;
    The like he ne'er saw wi' his e'e!
On the fore front o' that castle fair,
    Twa unicorns were gay to see;
The picture of a knight, and a lady bright,
    And the green hollin abune their brie.

Thereat he spied five hundred men,
    Shooting with bows on Newark Lee;
They were a' in ae livery clad,
    O' the Linkome green sae gay to see.

His men were a' clad in the green,
    The knight was armed capapie,
With a bended bow, on a milk-white steed;
    And I wot they ranked right bonnily.

Thereby Boyd kend he was master man,
    And served him in his ain degree.
'God mot thee save, brave Outlaw Murray!
    Thy lady and all thy chivalry!'

'Marry, thou's welcome, gentleman,
    Some King's messenger thou seems to be.'

'The King of Scotland sent me here,
    And, good Outlaw, I am sent to thee;
I wad wot of whom ye hold your lands,
    Or man, wha may thy master be?'

'Thir lands are MINE!' the Outlaw said;
    I ken nae King in Christentie;
Frae Soudron I this Forest wan,
    Whan the King nor his knights were not to see.'

'He desires you'll come to Edinburgh,
    And hauld of him this Forest free;
And, if ye refuse to do this,
    He'll conquess baith thy lands and thee.
He hath vowed to cast thy castle down,
    And make a widow o' thy gay lady;

'He'll hang thy merrymen, pair by pair,
    In ony frith where he may them find.'
'Aye, by my troth!' the Outlaw said,
    'Than wald I think me far behind.

'Ere the King my fair country get,
    This land that's nativest to me!
Many o' his nobles sall be cauld,
    Their ladies sall be right weary.'

Then spak his lady, fair of face,
    She said, 'Without consent of me,
That an Outlaw suld come before a King;
    I am right rad of treasonrie.
Bid him be gude to his lords at hame,
    For Edinburgh my lord sall never see.'

James Boyd took his leave o' the Outlaw keen,
    To Edinburgh boun' is he;
When James he cam before the King,
    He knelit lowly on his knee.

'Welcome, James Boyd!' said our noble King;
    'What Forest is Ettrick Forest free?'
'Ettrick Forest is the fairest forest
    That ever man saw wi' his e'e.

'There's the dae, the rae, the hart, the hind,
    And of a' wild beastis great plenty;
There's a pretty castle of lime and stane,
    O if it stands not pleasantly!

'There's in the forefront o' that castle,
    Twa unicorns, sae bra' to see;
There's the picture of a knight, and a lady bright,
    Wi' the green hollin abune their brie.

'There the Outlaw keeps five hundred men,
    He keeps a royal company!
His merrymen in ae livery clad,
    O' the Linkome green sae gay to see.
He and his lady in purple clad;
    O! gin they live not royally!

'He says yon Forest is his awin;
    He wan it frae the Southronie;
Sae as he wan it, sae will he keep it,
    Contrair all kings in Christentie.'

'Gar warn me Perthshire, and Angus baith;
    Fife up and down, and the Lothians three,
And graith my horse!' said our noble King,
    'For to Ettrick Forest hie will I me.'

Then word is gane the Outlaw till,
    In Ettrick Forest, where dwelleth he,
That the King was coming to his country,
    To conquess baith his lands and he.

'I mak a vow,' the Outlaw said,
    'I mak a vow, and that truly,
Were there but three men to tak my pairt,
    Yon King's coming full dear should be!'

Then messengers he called forth,
    And bade them hie them speedily –
'Ane of ye gae to Halliday,
    The laird of the Corehead is he.

'He certain is my sister's son;
    Bid him come quick and succour me!
The King comes on for Ettrick Forest,
    And landless men we a' will be.'

'What news? What news?' said Halliday,
    'Man, frae thy master unto me?'
'Not as ye wad; seeking your aid;
    The King's his mortal enemy.'

'Aye, by troth!' said Halliday,
    'Even for that it repenteth me;
For if he lose fair Ettrick Forest,
    He'll tak fair Moffatdale frae me.

'I'll meet him wi' five hundred men,
    And surely mair, if mair may be;
And before he gets the Forest fair,
    We a' will die on Newark Lee!'

The Outlaw called a messenger,
    And bid him hie him speedily,
To Andrew Murray of Cockpool –
    'That man's a dear cousin to me;
Desire him come, and mak me aid,
    With a' the power that may be.'

'It stands me hard,' Andrew Murray said,
    'Judge if it stands na hard wi' me;
To enter against a King wi' crown,
    And set my lands in jeopardy!
Yet, if I come not on the day,
    Surely at night he sall me see.'

To Sir James Murray of Traquair,
    A message cam right speedily –
'What news? What news?' James Murray said,
    'Man, frae thy master unto me?'

'What needs I tell? For weel ye ken,
    The King's his mortal enemy;
And now he's coming to Ettrick Forest,
    And landless men ye a' will be.'

'And by my troth,' James Murray said,
    'Wi' that Outlaw will I live and die;
The King has gifted my lands lang syne –
    It cannot be nae warse wi' me.'

The King was coming through Caddon Ford,
    And full five thousand men was he;
They saw the dark Forest them before,
    They thought it awesome for to see.

Then spak the lord, hight Hamilton,
   And to the noble King said he,
'My sovereign liege, some counsel tak,
   First at your nobles, syne at me.

'Desire him meet thee at Permanscore,
   And bring four in his company;
Five earle sall gang yoursell before,
   Gude cause that you should honoured be.

'And if he refuses to do that,
   We'll conquess baith his lands and he;
There sall never a Murray, after him,
   Hald land in Ettrick Forest free.'

Then spak the keen Laird of Buckscleuth,
   A stalwart man, and stern was he –
'For a King to gang an Outlaw till,
   Is beneath his state and dignity.

'The man that wons yon Forest intill,
   He lives by reif and felony!
Wherefore, brayd on, my sovereign liege!
   Wi' fire and sword we'll follow thee;
Or, if your courtrie lords fa' back,
   Our Borderers sall the onset gie.'

Then out and spak the noble King,
   And round him cast a wily e'e –
'Now had thy tongue Sir Walter Scott,
   Nor speak of reif nor felony:
For, had every honest man his awin kye,
   A right puir clan thy name wad be!'

The King then called a gentleman,
  Royal banner-bearer there was he;
James Hoppringle of Torsonse by name;
  He cam and knelt upon his knee.

'Welcome, James Pringle of Torsonse!
  A message ye maun gang for me;
Ye maun gae to yon Outlaw Murray,
  Surely where bauldly bideth he.

'Bid him meet me at Permanscore,
  And bring four in his company;
Five earls sall come wi' mysel,
  Gude reason I suld honoured be.

'And, if he refuses to do that,
  Bid him look for nae good o' me!
There sall never a Murray after him,
  Have land in Ettrick Forest free.'

James came before the Outlaw keen,
  And served him in his ain degree –
'Welcome, James Pringle of Torsonse!
  What message frae the King to me?'

'He bids ye meet him at Permanscore,
  And bring four in your company;
Five earls sall gang himsell before,
  Nae mair in number will he be.

'And if you refuse to do that,
  (I freely here upgive wi' thee)
He'll cast yon bonny castle down,
  And make a widow o' that gay lady.

'He'll loose yon bluidhound Borderers,
    Wi' fire and sword to follow thee;
There will never a Murray, after thysell,
    Have land in Ettrick Forest free.'

'It stands me hard,' the Outlaw said;
    'Judge if it stands na hard wi' me!
Wha reck not losing of mysell,
    But a' my offspring after me.

'My merrymen's lives, my widow's tears –
    There lies the pang that pinches me!
When I am straught in bluidy eard,
    Yon castle will be right dreary.

'Auld Halliday, young Halliday,
    Ye sall be twa to gang wi' me;
Andrew Murray, and Sir James Murray,
    We'll be nae mae in company.'

When that they cam before the King,
    They fell before him on their knee –
'Grant mercy, mercy, noble King!
    E'en for his sake that died on tree.'

'Sicken like mercy sall ye have;
    On gallows ye sall hangit be!'
'Over God's forbode,' quoth the Outlaw then,
    'I hope your grace will better be!
Else, ere you come to Edinburgh port,
    I trow thin guarded sall ye be:

'Thir lands of Ettrick Forest fair,
    I wan them from the enemy;
Like as I wan them, sae will I keep them,
    Contrair all kings in Christentie.'

All the nobles the King about,
    Said pity it were to see him die –
'Yet graunt me mercy, sovereign prince!
    Extend your favour unto me!

'I'll give thee the keys of my castle,
    Wi' the blessing o' my gay lady,
Gin thou'lt make me sheriff of this Forest,
    And a' my offspring after me.'

'Wilt thou give me the keys of thy castle,
    Wi' the blessing of thy gay lady?
I'se make thee sheriff of Ettrick Forest,
    Surely while upward grows the tree;
If you be not traitor to the King,
    Forfaulted sall thou never be.'

'But, Prince, what sall come o' my men?
    When I gae back, traitor they'll ca' me.
I had rather lose my life and land,
    Ere my merrymen rebuked me.'

'Will your merrymen amend their lives?
    And a' their pardons I grant thee –
Now, name thy lands where'er they lie,
    And here I RENDER them to thee.'

'Fair Philiphaugh is mine by right,
    And Lewinshope still mine sall be;
Newark, Foulshiells, and Tinnies baith,
    My bow and arrow purchased me.

'And I have native steads to me,
    The Newark Lee and Hangingshaw;
I have mony steads in the Forest shaw,
    But them by name I dinna knaw.'

The keys o' the castle gave he the king,
    Wi' the blessing o' his fair lady;
He was made sheriff of Ettrick Forest,
    Surely while upward grows the tree;
And if he was na traitor to the King,
    Forfaulted he suld never be.

Wha ever heard, in ony times,
    Sicken an Outlaw in his degree,
Sic favour get before a King,
    As did the OUTLAW MURRAY of the Forest free?

# THE DEATH OF PARCY REED
## [Child 193]

Taken down by James Telfer, a schoolmaster of Saughtree, Liddes-
dale, from Kitty Hall, a native of Redesdale. In a letter of 1844 to
Robert White of Newcastle, Telfer writes of the first three stanzas:
'If Mr White thinks proper he may prefix the above as the begin-
ning of the ballad. The verses are not very good; thay are written
*currente calamo.*' Telfer had sent a copy to Scott in 1824.

Parcy Reed: commonly believed to have been a Warden, but I
have found no record to support this.

Hingin' stane: hanging stone; a large leaning boulder, not a
place of execution.


God send the land deliverance
    Frae every reaving, riding Scot;
We'll sune hae neither cow nor ewe,
    We'll sune hae neither staig nor stot.

The outlaws come frae Liddesdale,
    They herry Redesdale far and near;
The rich man's gelding it maun gang,
    They canna pass the puir man's mear.

Sure it were weel, had ilka thief
    Around his neck a halter strang;
And curses heavy may they light
    On traitors vile oursels amang.

Now Parcy Reed has Crosier ta'en,
    He has delivered him to the law;
But Crosier says he'll do waur than that,
    He'll make the tower o' Troughend fa'.

And Crosier says he will do waur,
    He will do waur if waur can be;
He'll make the bairns a' fatherless,
    And then, the land it may lie lee.

'To the hunting, ho!' cried Parcy Reed,
    'The morning sun is on the dew;
The cauler breeze frae off the fells
    Will lead the dogs to the quarry true.

'To the hunting, ho!' cried Parcy Reed,
    And to the hunting he has gane;
And the three fause Ha's o' Girsonsfield
    Alang wi' him he has them ta'en.

They hunted high, they hunted low,
    By heathery hill and birken shaw;
They raised a buck on Rooken Edge,
    And blew the mort at fair Ealylawe.

They hunted high, they hunted low,
    They made the echoes ring amain;
With music sweet o' horn and hound,
    They merry made fair Redesdale glen.

They hunted high, they hunted low,
    They hunted up, they hunted down,
Until the day was past the prime,
    And it grew late in the afternoon.

They hunted high in Batinghope,
    When as the sun was sinking low;
Says Parcy then, 'Ca' off the dogs,
    We'll bait our steeds and homeward go.'

They lighted high in Batinghope,
    Atween the brown and benty ground;
They had but rested a little while
    Till Parcy Reed was sleeping sound.

There's nane may lean on a rotten staff,
    But him that riŝks to get a fa';
There's nane may in a traitor trust,
    And traitors black were every Ha'.

They've stown the bridle off his steed,
    And they've put water in his lang gun;
They've fixed his sword within the sheath
    That out again it winna come.

'Awaken ye, waken ye, Parcy Reed,
    Or by your enemies be ta'en;
For yonder are the five Crosiers
    A-coming owre the Hingin-stane.'

'If they be five, and we be four,
    Sae that ye stand alang wi' me,
Then every man ye will take one,
    And only leave but two to me:
We will them meet as brave men ought,
    And make them either fight or flee.'

'We mayna stand, we canna stand,
    We daurna stand alang wi' thee;
The Crosiers haud thee at a feud,
    And they wad kill baith thee and we.'

'O turn thee, turn thee, Johnie Ha',
    O turn thee, man, and fight wi' me;
When ye come to Troughend again,
    My gude black naig I will gie thee;

He cost full twenty pound o' gowd,
    Atween my brother John and me.'

'I mayna turn, I canna turn,
    I daurna turn and fight wi' thee;
The Crosiers haud thee at a feud,
    And they wad kill baith thee and me.'

'O turn thee, turn thee, Willie Ha',
    O turn thee, man, and fight wi' me;
When ye come to Troughend again,
    A yoke o' owsen I'll gie thee.'

'I mayna turn, I canna turn,
    I daurna turn and fight wi' thee;
The Crosiers haud thee at a feud,
    And they wad kill baith thee and me.'

'O turn thee, turn thee, Tommy Ha',
    O turn now, man, and fight wi' me;
If ever we come to Troughend again,
    My daughter Jean I'll gie to thee.'

'I mayna turn, I canna turn,
    I daurna turn and fight wi' thee;
The Crosiers haud thee at a feud,
    And they wad kill baith thee and me.'

'O shame upon ye, traitors a'!
    I wish your hames ye may never see;
Ye've stown the bridle off my naig,
    And I can neither fight nor flee.

'Ye've stown the bridle off my naig,
    And ye've put water i' my lang gun;

Ye've fixed my sword within the sheath
    That out again it winna come.'

He had but time to cross himsel,
    A prayer he hadna time to say,
Till round him came the Crosiers keen,
    All riding graithed and in array.

'Weel met, weel met, now, Parcy Reed,
    Thou art the very man we sought;
Owre lang hae we been in your debt,
    Now we will pay you as we ought.

'We'll pay thee at the nearest tree,
    Where we shall hang thee like a hound;'
Brave Parcy raised his fankit sword,
    And felled the foremost to the ground.

Alack, and wae for Parcy Reed,
    Alack, he was an unarmed man;
Four weapons pierced him all at once,
    As they assailed him there and than.

They fell upon him all at once,
    They mangled him most cruelly;
The slightest wound might caused his deid,
    And they hae gi'en him thirty-three;
They hacket off his hands and feet,
    And left him lying on the lee.

'Now, Parcy Reed, we've paid our debt,
    Ye canna weel dispute the tale,'
The Crosiers said, and off they rade;
    They rade the airt o' Liddesdale.

It was the hour o' gloaming gray,
    When herds come in frae fauld and pen;
A herd he saw a huntsman lie,
    Says he, 'Can this be Laird Troughen'?'

'There's some will ca' me Parcy Reed,
    And some will ca' me Laird Troughen';
It's little matter what they ca' me,
    My faes has made me ill to ken.

'There's some will ca' me Parcy Reed,
    And speak my praise in tower and town;
It's little matter what they do now,
    My life-blood rudds the heather brown.

'There's some will ca' me Parcy Reed,
    And a' my virtues say and sing;
I would much rather have just now
    A draught of water from the spring.'

The herd flung off his clouted shoon
    And to the nearest fountain ran;
He made his bonnet serve a cup,
    And wan the blessing o' the dying man.

'Now, honest herd, ye maun do mair,
    Ye maun do mair, as I you tell;
Ye maun bear tidings to Troughend,
    And bear likewise my last farewell.

'A farewell to my wedded wife,
    A farewell to my brother John,
Wha sits into the Troughend tower
    Wi' heart as black as any stone.

'A farewell to my daughter Jean,
    A farewell to my young sons five;
Had they been at their father's hand,
    I had this night been man alive.

'A farewell to my followers a',
    And a' my neighbours good at need;
Bid them think how the treacherous Ha's
    Betrayed the life o' Parcy Reed.

'The Laird o' Clennel bears my bow,
    The Laird o' Brandon bears my brand;
Whene'er they ride i' the Border-side,
    They'll mind the fate o' the Laird Troughend.'

# THE RAID OF THE REIDSWIRE

*[Minstrelsy]*

The incident occurred on 7 July 1575.

    Carmichael: Keeper of Liddesdale.

    Armestranges: 'not a hail' (whole) family, because outlawed.

    Hearoune: Sir George Heron, Forster's brother-in-law, Deputy, and Keeper of Redesdale.

    Farnstein: a Robson of Falstone, N. Tyne.


The seventh of July, the suith to say,
    At the Reidswire the tryst was set;
Our wardens they affixed the day,
    And, as they promised, so they met.
    Alas! that day I'll ne'er forget!
Was sure sae feard, and then sae fain –
    They came there justice for to get,
Will never green to come again.

Carmichael was our warden then,
    He caused the country to convene;
And the Laird's Wat, that worthy man,
    Brought in that surname weil beseen:
    The Armestrangs, that aye hae been
A hardie house, but not a hail,
    The Elliot's honours to maintain,
Brought down the lave o' Liddesdale.

Then Tividale came to wi' speed;
    The sheriff brought the Douglas down,
Wi' Cranstane, Gladstain, good at need,
    Baith Rule water and Hawick town.
    Beanjeddart bauldly made him boun,
Wi' a' the Trumbills strong and stout;
    The Rutherfords, with great renown,
Convoyed the town of Jedburgh out.

Of other clans I cannot tell,
    Because our warning was not wide. –
Be this our folks hae ta'en the fell,
    And planted down pallions there to bide.
    We looked down the other side,
And saw come breasting owre the brae,
    Wi' Sir John Forster for their guide,
Full fifteen hundred men and mae.

It grieved him sair, that day, I trow,
    Wi' Sir George Hearoune of Schipsydehouse:
Because we were not men enow,
    They counted us not worth a louse.
    Sir George was gentle, meek, and douse,
But *he* was hail and het as fire;
    And yet, for all his cracking crouse,
He rewed the raid o' the Reidswire.

To deal with proud men is but pain;
    For either must ye fight or flee,
Or else no answer make again,
    But play the beast, and let them be.
    It was na wonder he was hie,
Had Tindale, Redesdale, at his hand,
    Wi' Cukdale, Gladsdale on the lee,
And Hebsrime, and Northumberland.

Yet was our meeting meek enough,
    Begun wi' merriment and mowes,
And at the brae, aboon the heugh,
    The clerk sat down to call the rowes,
    And some for kine, and some for ewes,
Called in of Dandrie, Hob, and Jock –
    We saw, come marching ower the knows,
Five hundred Fenwicks in a flock.

With jack and spear, and bows all bent,
    And warlike weapons at their will:
Although we were na well content,
    Yet be my troth we feard no ill.
    Some gaed to drink, and some stude still,
And some to cards and dice them sped;
    Till on ane Farnstein they filed a bill,
And he was fugitive and fled.

Carmichael bade them speak out plainly,
    And cloak no cause for ill nor good;
The other, answering him as vainly,
    Began to reckon kin and blood:
    He raise, and raxed him where he stood,
And bade him match him with his marrows,
    Then Tindale heard them reason rude,
And they loot off a flight of arrows.

Then was there nought but bow and spear,
    And every man pulled out a brand;
'A Schafton and a Fenwick' there:
    Good Symington was slain frae hand.
    The Scotsmen cried on other to stand,
Frae time they saw John Robson slain –
    What should they cry? the King's command
Could cause no cowards turn again.

Up rose the laird to red the cumber,
    Which would not be for all his boast;
What could we do with sic a number?
    Five thousand men into a host.
    Then Henry Purdie proved his cost,
And very narrowly had mischiefed him,
    And there we had our warden lost,
Wer't not the grit God he relieved him.

Another through the breeks him bair,
    While flatlies to the ground he fell:
Than thought I weel we had lost him there,
    Into my stomach it struck a knell!
    Yet up he raise the truth to tell ye,
And laid about him dints full dour;
    His horsemen they rade sturdily,
And stood about him in the stour.

Then raise the slogan with ane shout –
    'Fy Tindale to it! Jedburgh's here!'
I trow he was not half sae stout,
    But ance his stomach was astir.
    With gun and genzie, bow and spear,
Men might see mony a cracked crown!
    But up amang the merchant gear,
They were as busy as we were down.

The swallow tail frae tackles flew,
    Five hundred flain into a flight,
But we had pistolets enow,
    And shot among them as we might.
    With help of God the game gaed right,
Frae time the foremost of them fell;
    Then ower the know, without goodnight,
They ran with many a shout and yell.

But after they had turned backs,
    Yet Tindale men they turned again;
And had not been the merchant packs,
    There had been mae of Scotland slain.
    But, Jesu! if the folks were fain
To put the bussing on their thighs;
    And so they fled, wi' a' their main,
Down ower the brae, like clogged bees.

Sir Francis Russell ta'en was there,
 And hurt, as we hear men rehearse;
Proud Wallington was wounded sair,
 Albeit he be a Fenwick fierce.
 But if ye wad a soldier search,
Among them a' were ta'en that night,
 Was nane sae wordie to put in verse,
As Collingwood, that courteous knight.

Young Henry Schafton, he is hurt;
 A soldier shot him wi' a bow:
Scotland has cause to make great sturt,
 For laming of the laird of Mow.
 The Laird's Wat did weel indeed;
His friends stood stoutly by himsel',
 With little Gladstain, good in need,
For Gretein kend na good be ill.

The Sheriff wanted not good will,
 Howbeit he might not fight so fast;
Beanjeddart, Hundlie, and Hunthill,
 Three, on they laid weel at the last.
 Except the horsemen of the guard,
If I could put men to avail,
 None stoutlier stood out for their laird
Nor did the lads of Liddesdale.

But little harness had we there;
 But auld Badreule had on a jack,
And did right weel, I you declare,
 With all his Trumbills at his back.
 Good Edderstane was not to lack,
Nor Kirktoun, Newton, noble men!
 Thirs all the specials I of speak,
By others that I could not ken.

Who did invent that day of play,
    We need not fear to find him soon;
For Sir John Forster, I dare well say,
    Made us this noisome afternoon.
    Not that I speak precisely out,
That he supposed it would be peril;
    But pride, and breaking out of feud,
Garr'd Tindale lads begin the quarrel.

# THE BATTLE OF OTTERBURN
*[Child 161A]*

This Northumbrian version is the earliest extant ballad record (early sixteenth century) of the battle in 1388.

Hoppertope: Ottercops.

Rodclyffe: Rothley

Styrand many a stage: correctly, many a styrand stage, i.e. many a lively march.

The blodye hart: the Douglas coat of arms includes 'a man's heart gules'.

Mark hym to the Trinity: make the sign of the cross.

Marked them one owre: took aim at.


It fell about the Lammas tide,
    When husbands wins their hay,
The doughty Douglas bound him to ride,
    In England to take a prey.

The Earl of Fife, withouten strife,
    He bound him over Solway;
The great would ever together ride:
    That raid they may rue for aye.

Over Hoppertope Hill they cam in,
    And so down by Rodclyffe crag:
Upon Green Linton they lighted down
    Styrand many a stage.

And boldly brent Northumberland,
    And harried many a town;
They did our English men great wrang,
    To battle that were not bound.

Then spake a berne upon the bent,
    Of comfort that was not cold,
And said, 'We have brent Northumberland,
    We have all wealth in hold.

'Now we have harried all Bamburgh shire,
    All the wealth in the world have we,
I rede we ride to New Castle,
    So still and stalworthly.'

Upon the morrow when it was day,
    The standards shone full bright;
To New Castle they took the way,
    And thither they cam full right.

Sir Henry Percy lay at the New Castle
    I tell you withouten drede;
He had been a march-man all his days,
    And kept Berwick upon Tweed.

To the New Castle when they cam,
    The Scots they cried on height,
'Sir Harry Percy, and thou byste within,
    Come to the fylde and fight

'For we have brent Northumberland,
    Thy heritage good and right,
And syne my lodging I have take
    With my brand dubbed many a knight.'

Sir Harry Percy cam to the walls
    The Scottish host for to see,
And said, 'And thou hast brent Northumberland,
    Full sore it reweth me.

'If thou hast harried all Bamburgh shire,
    Thou hast done me great envye;
For the trespass thou hast me done,
    The tone of us shall die.'

'Where shall I bide thee?' said the Douglas,
    'Or where wilt thou come to me?'
'At Otterburn, in the high way,
    There may'st thou well lodged be.

'The roe full reckless there she rins
    To make thee game and glee;
The falcon and the pheasant both,
    Among the holts on high.

'There may'st thou have thy wealth at will,
    Well lodged there may'st be;
It shall not be long or I come thee till,'
    Said Sir Harry Percy.

'There shall I bide thee,' said the Douglas,
    'By the faith of my body:'
'Thither shall I come,' said Sir Harry Percy,
    'My troth I plight to thee.'

A pipe of wine he gave them over the walls,
    For sooth as I you say;
There he made the Douglas drink,
    And all his host that day.

The Douglas turned him homeward again,
    For sooth withouten nay;
He took his lodging at Otterburn,
    Upon a Wednesday.

And there he pight his standard down,
　　His getting more and less,
And syne he warned his men to go
　　To choose their geldings gress.

A Scottish knight hoved upon the bent,
　　A watch I dare well say;
So was he ware on the noble Percy,
　　In the dawning of the day.

He pricked to his pavilion door,
　　As fast as he might run;
'Awaken, Douglas,' cried the knight,
　　'For his love that sits on throne.

'Awaken, Douglas,' cried the knight,
　　'For thou may'st waken with winne;
Yonder have I spied the proud Percy,
　　And seven standards with him.'

'Nay, by my troth,' the Douglas said,
　　'It is but a fained tale;
He durst not look on my brede banner
　　For all England so hale.

'Was I not yesterday at the New Castle,
　　That stands so fair on Tyne?
For all the men that Percy had,
　　He could not gar me once to dine.'

He stepped out at his pavilion door,
　　To look and it were less:
'Array now, lordings, one and all,
　　For here begins no peace.

'The Earl of Mentaye, thou art my eme,
    The forward I give to thee:
The Earl of Huntlay, cawte and keen,
    He shall be with thee.

'The Lord of Buchan, in armour bright,
    On the other hand he shall be;
Lord Johnston and Lord Maxwell,
    They too shall be with me.

Swynton, fair fylde upon your pride!
    To battle make you bound
Sir Davy Scott, Sir Walter Stewarde,
    Sir John of Agurstone!'

The Percy came before his host,
    Which was ever a gentle knight;
Upon the Douglas loud can he cry,
    'I will hold that I have hight.

'For thou hast brent Northumberland,
    And done me great envye;
For this trespass thou hast me done,
    The tone of us shall die.'

The Douglas answered him again,
    With great words upon high,
And said, 'I have twenty against thy one,
    Behold, and thou may'st see.'

With that the Percy was grieved sore,
    For sooth as I you say;
He lighted down upon his foot,
    And shoot his horse clean away.

Every man saw that he did so,
    That royal was ever in rout;
Every man shoot his horse him fro,
    And light him round about.

Thus Sir Harry Percy took the field,
    For sooth as I yóu say;
Jesu Christ in heaven on hight
    Did help him well that day.

But nine thousand, there was no more,
    The chronicle will not layne;
Forty thousand of Scots and four
    That day fought them again.

But when the battle began to join,
    In haste there cam a knight;
The letters fair forth he hath ta'en,
    And thus he said full right:

'My lord your father he greets you well,
    With many a noble knight;
He desires you to bide
    That he may see this fight.

The Baron of Greystoke is come out of the west,
    With him a noble company;
All they lodge at your father's this night,
    And the battle fain would they see.'

'For Jesus love,' said Sir Harry Percy,
    'That died for you and me,
Wend to my lord my father again,
    And say ye saw me not with ye.

'My troth is plight to yon Scottish knight,
    It needs me not to layne,
That I should bide him on this bent,
    And I have his troth again.

'And if that I wend off this ground,
    For sooth, unfoughten away,
He would me call but a coward knight
    In his land another day.

'Yet had I liefer to be rived and rent,
    By Mary that mickle maye,
Than ever my manhood should be reproved
    With a Scot another day.

'Wherefore shoot, archers, for my sake,
    And let sharp arrows flee;
Minstrels, play up for your warison,
    And well quit it shall be.

'Every man think on his true-love,
    And mark him to the Trinity;
For to God I make mine avow
    This day will I not flee.'

The bloody heart in the Douglas arms,
    His standard stood on high,
That every man might full well know;
    By side stood starres three.

The white lion on the English part,
    For sooth as I you sayne,
The lucettes and the crescents both;
    The Scots fought them again.

Upon Saint Andrew loud can they cry,
    And thrice they shout on hight,
And syne marked them one owre English men,
    As I have told you right.

Saint George the bright, our lady's knight,
    To name they were full fain;
Our English men they cried on hight,
    And thrice they shout again.

With that sharp arrows began to flee,
    I tell you in certain;
Men of arms began to join
    Many a doughty man was there slain.

The Percy and the Douglas met,
    That either of other was fain;
They swapped together while that they sweat,
    With swords of fine collayne:

Till the blood from their bassonets ran,
    As the roke doth in the rain;
'Yield thee to me,' said the Douglas,
    'Or else thou shalt be slain.

'For I see by thy bright bassonet,
    Thou art some man of might:
And so I do by thy burnished brand;
    Thou art an earl, or else a knight.'

'By my good faith,' said the noble Percy,
    'Now hast thou rede full right;
Yet will I never yield me to thee,
    While I may stand and fight.'

They swapped together while that they sweat,
　　With swordës sharp and long;
Each on other so fast they beat,
　　Till their helms cam in pieces down.

The Percy was a man of strength,
　　I tell you in this stounde;
He smote the Douglas at the swordës length
　　That he fell to the ground.

The sword was sharp, and sore can bite,
　　I tell you in certain;
To the heart he could him smite,
　　Thus was the Douglas slain.

The standards stood still on eke a side,
　　With many a grievous groan;
There they fought the day, and all the night,
　　And many a doughty man was slain.

There was no freke that there would fly,
　　But stiffly in stour can stand,
Each one hewing on other while they might drye,
　　With many a baleful brand.

There was slain upon the Scottës side,
　　For sooth and certainly,
Sir James a Douglas there was slain,
　　That day that he could die.

The Earl of Mentaye he was slain,
　　Grisly groaned upon the ground;
Sir Davy Scott, Sir Walter Stewarde,
　　Sir John of Agurstone.

Sir Charles Morrey in that place,
    That never a foot would flee;
Sir Hugh Maxwell, a lord he was,
    With the Douglas he did die.

There was slain upon the Scottës side,
    For sooth as I you say,
Of four and forty thousand Scots,
    Went but eighteen away.

There was slain upon the English side,
    For sooth and certainly,
A gentle knight, Sir John Fitzhugh,
    It was the more pity.

Sir James Harbottle there was slain,
    For him their hearts were sore;
The gentle Lovell there was slain,
    That the Percy's standard bore.

There was slain upon the English part,
    For sooth as I you say,
Of nine thousand English men
    Five hundred came away.

The other were slain in the field;
    Christ keep their souls from woe!
Seeing there was so few friends
    Against so many a foe.

Then on the morn they made them biers
    Of birch and hazel gray;
Many a widow, with weeping tears,
    Their makes they fette away.

This fray began at Otterburn,
    Between the night and the day;
There the Douglas lost his life,
    And the Percy was led away.

Then was there a Scottish prisoner ta'en,
    Sir Hugh Montgomery was his name;
For sooth as I you say,
    He borrowed Percy home again.

Now let us all for the Percy pray
    To Jesu most of might,
To bring his soul to the bliss of heaven,
    For he was a gentle knight.

# BALLADS OF THE MIDDLE MARCHES (2)
## Romance

# THE DOUGLAS TRAGEDY
## [Child 7B]

Traditionally, a tale of Blackhouse Tower on the Douglas Burn in the Yarrow Valley.


'Rise up, rise up, now, Lord Douglas,' she says,
    'And put on your armour so bright;
Let it never be said that a daughter of thine
    Was married to a lord under night.

'Rise up, rise up, my seven bold sons,
    And put on your armour so bright,
And take better care of your youngest sister,
    For your eldest's awa the last night.'

He's mounted her on a milk-white steed,
    And himself on a dapple grey,
With a bugelet horn hung down by his side,
    And lightly they rode away.

Lord William lookit o'er his left shoulder,
    To see what he could see,
And there he spy'd her seven brethren bold,
    Come riding over the lee.

'Light down, light down, Lady Marg'ret,' he said,
    'And hold my steed in your hand,
Until that against your seven brethren bold,
    And your father, I mak a stand.'

She held his steed in her milk-white hand,
    And never shed one tear,
Until that she saw her seven brethren fa',
    And her father hard fighting, who lov'd her so dear.

'O hold your hand, Lord William!' she said,
    'For your strokes they are wondrous sair;
True lovers I can get many a ane,
    But a father I can never get mair.'

O she's ta'en out her handkerchief,
    It was o' the holland sae fine,
And aye she dighted her father's bloody wounds,
    That were redder than the wine.

'O chuse, O chuse, Lady Marg'ret,' he said,
    'O whether will ye gang or bide?'
'I'll gang, I'll gang, Lord William,' she said,
    'For ye have left me no other guide.'

He's lifted her on a milk-white steed,
    And himself on a dapple grey,
With a bugelet horn hung down by his side,
    And slowly they baith rade away.

O they rade on, and on they rade,
    And a' by the light of the moon,
Until they came to yon wan water,
    And there they lighted down.

They lighted down to tak a drink
    Of the spring that ran sae clear;
And down the stream ran his gude heart's blood,
    And sair she gan to fear.

'Hold up, hold up, Lord William,' she says,
    'For I fear that you are slain!'
''Tis naething but the shadow of my scarlet cloak,
    That shines in the water sae plain.'

O they rade on, and on they rade,
　　And a' by the light of the moon,
Until they cam to his mother's ha' door,
　　And there they lighted down.

'Get up, get up, lady mother,' he says,
　　'Get up, and let me in! –
Get up, get up, lady mother,' he says,
　　'For this night my fair ladye I've win.

'O mak my bed, lady mother,' he says,
　　'O mak it braid and deep!
And lay Lady Marg'ret close at my back,
　　And the sounder I will sleep.'

Lord William was dead lang ere midnight,
　　Lady Marg'ret lang ere day –
And all true lovers that go thegither,
　　May they have mair luck than they!

Lord William was buried in St Mary's kirk,
　　Lady Marg'ret in Mary's quire;
Out o' the lady's grave grew a bonny red rose,
　　And out o' the knight's a brier.

And they twa met, and they twa plat,
　　And fain they wad be near;
And a' the warld might ken right weel,
　　They were twa lovers dear.

But bye and rade the Black Douglas,
　　And wow but he was rough!
For he pull'd up the bonny brier,
　　And flang't in St Mary's Loch.

# THE DOWIE DENS OF YARROW
## [Child 241E]


Late at e'en, drinking the wine,
    And ere they paid the lawing,
They set a combat them between,
    To fight it in the dawing.

'O stay at hame, my noble lord!
    O stay at hame, my marrow!
My cruel brother will you betray
    On the dowie houms of Yarrow.'

'O fare ye weel, my ladye gaye!
    O fare ye weel, my Sarah!
For I maun gang, though I ne'er return,
    Frae the dowie banks o' Yarrow.'

She kissed his cheek, she kaimed his hair,
    As oft she had done before, O;
She belted him with his noble brand,
    And he's awa' to Yarrow.

As he gaed up the Tennies bank,
    I wot he gaed wi' sorrow,
Till, down in a den, he spied nine arm'd men,
    On the dowie houms of Yarrow.

'O come ye here to part your land,
    The bonnie Forest thorough?
Or come ye here to wield your brand,
    On the dowie houms of Yarrow?'

'I come not here to part my land,
    And neither to beg nor borrow;
I come to wield my noble brand,
    On the bonnie banks of Yarrow.

'If I see all, ye're nine to ane;
    And that's an unequal marrow;
Yet will I fight, while lasts my brand,
    On the bonnie banks of Yarrow.'

Four has he hurt, and five has slain,
    On the bloody braes of Yarrow,
Till that stubborn knight came him behind,
    And ran his body thorough.

'Gae hame, gae hame, good-brother John,
    And tell your sister Sarah,
To come and lift her leafu' lord;
    He's sleepin sound on Yarrow.' –

Yestreen I dream'd a dolefu' dream;
    I fear there will be sorrow!
I dream'd I pu'd the heather green,
    Wi' my true love, on Yarrow.

'O gentle wind, that bloweth south,
    From where my love repaireth,
Convey a kiss from his dear mouth,
    And tell me how he fareth!

'But in the glen strive armed men;
    They've wrought me dole and sorrow;
They've slain – the comeliest knight they've slain –
    He bleeding lies on Yarrow.'

As she sped down yon high high hill,
  She gaed wi' dole and sorrow,
And in the glen spyed ten slain men,
  On the dowie banks of Yarrow.

She kissed his cheek, she kaimed his hair,
  She searched his wounds all thorough;
She kissed them, till her lips grew red,
  On the dowie houms of Yarrow.

'Now haud your tongue, my daughter dear!
  For a' this breeds but sorrow;
I'll wed ye to a better lord
  Than him ye lost on Yarrow.'

'O haud your tongue, my father dear!
  Ye mind me but of sorrow;
A fairer rose did never bloom
  Than now lies cropp'd on Yarrow.'

# RARE WILLIE DROWNED IN YARROW
## [Child 215A]

'Willy's rare, and Willy's fair,
    And Willy's wondrous bonny,
And Willy heght tó marry me,
    Gin e'er he married ony.

'Yestreen I made my bed fu' brade,
    The night I'll make it narrow,
For a' the live-long winter's night
    I lie twin'd of my marrow.

'O came you by yon water-side?
    Pu'd you the rose or lilly?
Or came you by yon meadow green?
    Or saw you my sweet Willy?'

She sought him east, she sought him west,
    She sought him brade and narrow;
Sine, in the clifting of a craig,
    She found him drowned in Yarrow.

# THE LAMENT OF THE BORDER WIDOW
*[Child 106]*


My love he built me a bonny bower,
And clad it a' wi' lilye flour;
A brawer bower ye' ne'er did see,
Than my true love he built for me.

There came a man, by middle day,
He spied his sport and went away;
And brought the King that very night,
Who brake my bower and slew my knight.

He slew my knight, to me sae dear;
He slew my knight and poin'd his gear;
My servants all for life did flee,
And left me in extremitie.

I sew'd his sheet, making my mane;
I watched the corpse, myself alane;
I watched his body night and day;
No living creature came that way.

I took his body on my back,
And whiles I gaed, and whiles I sat;
I digg'd a grave, and laid him in,
And happ'd him with the sod sae green.

But think na ye my heart was sair,
When I laid the moul' on his yellow hair;
O think na ye my heart was wae,
When I turn'd about, away to gae?

Nae living man I'll love again,
Since that my lovely knight is slain;
Wi' ae lock of his yellow hair
I'll chain my heart for evermair.

# LAMKIN

*[Child 93 add.]*

Many versions of this story of an unpaid bill have been recorded on both sides of the Border. This one was given to Scott by James Hogg; it does not appear in the *Minstrelsy*.

Lamkin was as good a mason
 As ever liftit stane;
He built to the laird o' Lariston,
 But payment gat he nane.

Oft he came, an' ay he came,
 To that good lord's yett,
But neither at door nor window
 Ony entrance could get.

Till ae wae an' weary day
 Early he came,
An' it fell out on that day
 That good lord was frae hame.

He bade steek dor an' window,
 An' prick them to the gin,
Nor leave a little wee hole,
 Else Lamkin wad be in.

Noorice steekit dor an' window,
 She steekit them to the gin;
But she left a little wee hole
 That Lamkin might win in.

'O where's the lady o' this house?'
    Said cruel Lamkin;
'She's up the stair sleepin,'
    Said fause noorice then.

'How will we get her down the stair?'
    Said cruel Lamkin;
'We'll stogg the baby i' the cradle,'
    Said fause noorice then.

He stoggit, and she rockit,
    Till a' the floor swam,
An' a' the tors o' the cradle
    Red wi' blude ran.

'O still my son, noorice,
    O still him wi' the kane;'
'He winna still, madam,
    Till Lariston come hame.'

'O still my son, noorice,
    O still him wi' the knife;'
'I canna still him, madam,
    If ye sude tak my life.'

'O still my son, noorice,
    O still him wi' the bell;'
'He winna still, madam,
    Come see him yoursel.'

Wae an' weary rase she up,
    Slowly pat her on
Her green claethin' o' the silk,
    An' slowly came she down.

The first step she steppit,
    It was on a stone;
The first body she saw
    Was cruel Lamkin.

'O pity, pity, Lamkin,
    Hae pity on me!'
'Just as meikle pity, madam,
    As ye paid me o' my fee.'

'I'll gi' ye a peck o' good red goud,
    Streekit wi' the wand;
An' if that winna please ye,
    I'll heap it wi' my hand.

'An' if that winna please ye,
    O' goud an' o' fee,
I'll gi' ye my eldest daughter,
    Your wedded wife to be.'

'Gae wash the bason, lady,
    Gae wash 't an' mak it clean,
To kep your mother's heart's-blude,
    For she's of noble kin.'

'To kep my mother's heart'-blude
    I wad be right wae;
O tak mysel, Lamkin,
    An' let my mother gae.'

'Gae wash the bason, noorice,
    Gae wash 't an' mak it clean,
To kep your lady's heart's-blude,
    For she's o' noble kin.'

'To wash the bason, Lamkin,
    I will be right glad,
For mony, mony bursen day
    About her house I've had.'

But oh, what dule an' sorrow
    Was about that lord's ha',
When he fand his lady lyin'
    As white as driven snaw!

O what dule an' sorrow
    Whan that good lord cam in,
An' fand his young son murdered,
    I' the chimley lyin!

## THE CRUEL SISTER
*[Child 10C]*


There were two sisters sat in a bour;
    Binnorie, O Binnorie;
There came a knight to be their wooer;
    By the bonny milldams of Binnorie.

He courted the eldest with glove and ring,
But he lo'ed the youngest aboon a' thing.

He courted the eldest with broach and knife,
But he lo'ed the youngest aboon his life.

The eldest she was vexed sair,
And sore envied her sister fair.

The eldest said to the youngest ane,
'Will ye go and see our father's ships come in?'

She's ta'en her by the lilly hand,
And led her down to the river strand.

The youngest stude upon a stane,
The eldest came and pushed her in.

She took her by the middle sma',
And dashed her bonnie back to the jaw.

'O sister, sister, reach your hand,
And ye shall be heir of half my land.'

'O sister, I'll not reach my hand,
And I'll be heir of all your land.

'Shame fa' the hand that I should take,
It's twin'd me and my world's make.'

'O sister, reach me but your glove,
And sweet William shall be your love.'

'Sink on, nor hope for hand or glove,
And sweet William shall better be my love.

'Your cherry cheeks, your yellow hair
Garr'd me gang maiden evermair.'

Sometimes she sunk, and sometimes she swam,
Until she came to the miller's dam.

'O father, father, draw your dam,
There's either a mermaid or a milk-white swan.'

The miller hasted and drew his dam,
And there he found a drowned woman.

You could not see her yellow hair,
For gowd and pearls that were sae rare.

You could na see her middle sma',
Her gowden girdle was sae bra.

A famous harper passing by,
The sweet pale face he chanced to spy.

And when he looked that ladye on,
He sighed and made a heavy moan.

He made a harp of her breast-bone,
Whose sounds would melt a heart of stone.

The strings he framed of her yellow hair,
Whose notes made sad the listening ear.

He brought it to her father's hall,
And there was the court assembled all.

He laid his harp upon a stone,
And straight it began to play alone.

'O yonder sits my father, the king,
And yonder sits my mother, the queen.

'And yonder stands my brother Hugh,
And by him my William, sweet and true.'

But the last tune that the harp played then,
Was 'Woe to my sister, false Helen!'

# EDWARD
## *[Child 13B]*

'Why dois your brand sae drap wi' bluid,
     Edward, Edward,
Why dois your brand sae drap wi' bluid,
  And why sae sad gang yee O?'
'O I hae killed my hauke sae guid,
     Mither, mither,
O I hae killed my hauke sae guid,
  And I had nae mair bot hee, O.'

'Your haukis bluid was nevir sae reid,
     Edward, Edward,
Your haukis bluid was nevir sae reid,
  My deir son I tell thee O.'
'O I hae killed my reid-roan steid,
     Mither, mither,
O I hae killed my reid-roan steid,
  That erst was sae fair and frie O.'

'Your steid was auld, and ye hae gat mair,
     Edward, Edward,
Your steid was auld, and ye hae gat mair,
  Sum other dule ye drie O.'
'O I hae killed my fadir deir,
     Mither, mither,
O I hae killed my fadir deir,
  Alas and wae is me O!'

'And whatten penance wul ye drie, for that
     Edward, Edward?
And whatten penance wul ye drie for that?
  My deir son, now tell me O.'

'Ile set my feit in yonder boat,
        Mither, mither,
Ile set my feit in yonder boat,
    And I'll fare ovir the sea O.'

'And what wul ye doe wi' your towirs and your ha',
        Edward, Edward?
And what wul ye doe wi' your towirs and your ha',
    That were sae fair to see O?'
'Ile let thame stand tul they doun fa',
        Mither, mither,
Ile let thame stand tul they doun fa',
    For here nevir mair maun I bee O.'

'And what wul ye leive to your bairns and your wife,
        Edward, Edward?
And what wul ye leive to your bairns and your wife,
    Whan ye gang ovir the sea O?'
'The warldis room, late them beg thrae life,
    For thame nevir mair wul I see O.'

'And what wul ye leive to your ain mither dear,
        Edward, Edward?
And what wul ye leive to your ain mither dear?
    My deir son, now tell me O.'
'The curse of hell frae me sall ye beir,
        Mither, mither,
The curse of hell frae me sall ye beir,
    Sic counseils ye gave to me O.'

# LORD RANDAL
## [Child 12D]


'O where hae ye been, Lord Randal, my son?
O where hae ye been my handsome young man?'
'I hae been to the wild wood; mother, make my bed soon,
For I'm weary wi' hunting, and fain wald lie down.'

'Where gat ye your dinner, Lord Randal, my son?
Where gat ye your dinner, my handsome young man?
'I dined wi' my true-love; mother, make my bed soon,
For I'm weary wi' hunting, and fain wald lie down.'

'What gat ye to your dinner, Lord Randal, my son?
What gat ye to your dinner, my handsome young man?'
'I gat eels boiled in broo; mother, make my bed soon,
For I'm weary wi' hunting, and fain wald lie down.'

'What became of your bloodhounds, Lord Randal, my son?'
What became of your bloodhounds, my handsome young man?'
'O they swelled and they died; mother, make my bed soon,
For I'm weary wi' hunting, and fain wald lie down.'

'O I fear ye are poisoned, Lord Randal, my son!
O I fear ye are poisoned, my handsome young man!'
'O yes, I am poisoned, mother, make my bed soon,
For I'm sick at the heart, and I fain wald lie down.'

# THE TWA CORBIES
*[Minstrelsy]*

As I was walking all alane,
I heard twa corbies making a mane;
The tane unto the t'other say,
'Where sall we gang and dine to-day?'

'In behint yon auld fail dyke,
I wot there lies a new-slain knight;
And naebody kens that he lies there,
But his hawk, his hound, and lady fair.

'His hound is to the hunting gane,
His hawk to fetch the wild-fowl hame,
His lady's ta'en another mate,
So we may make our dinner sweet.

'Ye'll sit on his white hause-bane,
And I'll pike out his bonny blue een:
Wi' ae lock o' his gowden hair,
We'll theek our nest when it grows bare.

'Mony a one for him makes mane,
But nane sall ken where he is gane:
O'er his white banes, when they are bare,
The wind sall blaw for evermair.'

# THE FLOWER OF NORTHUMBERLAND
## *[Child 9E]*

This 'traditional version from the English border has unfortunately been improved by some literary pen' – Child.


A bailiff's daughter, she lived by the Aln,
    A young maid's love is easily won
She heard a poor prisoner making his moan,
    And she was the flower of Northumberland.

'If ye could love me, as I do love thee,
    A young maid's love is hard to win
I'll make you a lady of high degree,
    When once we go down to fair Scotland.'

To think of the prisoner her heart was sore,
    A young maid's love is easily won
Her love it was much, but her pity was more,
    And she was the flower of Northumberland.

She stole from her father's pillow the key,
And out of the dungeon she soon set him free,
    And she was the flower of Northumberland.

She led him into her father's stable,
And they've taken a steed both gallant and able,
    To carry them down to fair Scotland.

When they first took the way, it was darling and dear;
As forward they fared, all changed was his cheer,
    And she was the flower of Northumberland.

They rode till they came to a fair Scottish corse;
Says he, 'Now, pray madam, dismount from my horse,
     And go get you back to Northumberland.

'It befits not to ride with a leman light,
When awaits my returning my own lady bright,
     My own wedded wife in fair Scotland.'

The words that he said on her fond heart smote,
She knew not in sooth if she lived or not,
     And she was the flower of Northumberland.

She looked to his face, and it kythed so unkind
That her fast coming tears soon rendered her blind,
     And she was the flower of Northumberland.

'Have pity on me as I had it on thee,
     O why was my love so easily won!
A slave in your kitchen I'm willing to be,
     But I may not go back to Northumberland.

'Or carry me up by the middle sa sma',
     O why was my love so easily won!
And fling me headlong from your high castle wa',
     For I dare not go back to Northumberland.'

Her wailing, her woe, for nothing they went,
     A young maid's love is easily won
His bosom was stone and he would not relent,
     And she was the flower of Northumberland.

He turned him around and he thought of a plan,
He bought an old horse and hired an old man,
     To carry her back to Northumberland.

A heavy heart makes a weary way,
She reached her home in the evening gray,
　　　And she was the flower of Northumberland.

And all as she stood at her father's tower-gate,
More loud beat her heart than her knock thereat,
　　　And she was the flower of Northumberland.

Down came her step-dame, so rugged and doure,
　　　O why was your love so easily won!
'In Scotland go back to your false paramour,
　　　For you shall not stay here in Northumberland.'

Down came her father, he saw her and smiled,
　　　A young maid's love is easily won
'You are not the first that false Scots have beguiled,
　　　And ye're aye welcome back to Northumberland.

'You shall not want houses, you shall not want land,
You shall not want gold for to gain a husband,
　　　And ye're aye welcome back to Northumberland.'

# THE BROOM OF COWDENKNOWS
*[Child 217G]*

Cowdenknows is on the Leader Water between Earlston and
Melrose.

O the broom, and the bonny, bonny broom,
    And the broom of the Cowdenknows!
And aye sae sweet the lassie sang,
    I' the bought, milking the ewes.

The hills were high on ilka side,
    An' the bought i' the lirk o' the hill,
And aye, as she sang, her voice it rang
    Out-o'er the head o' yon hill.

There was a troop o' gentlemen
    Came riding merrilie by,
And one o' them has rode out o' the way,
    To the bought to the bonny may.

'Weel may ye save an' see, bonny lass,
    An weel may ye save an' see!'
'And sae wi' you, ye weel-bred knight,
    And what's your will wi' me?'

'The night is misty and mirk, fair may,
    And I have ridden astray,
And will ye be so kind, fair may,
    As come out and point my way?'

'Ride out, ride out, ye ramp rider!
    Your steed's baith stout and strang;
For out o' the bought I dare na come,
    For fear at ye do me wrang.'

'O winna ye pity me, bonny lass?
    O winna ye pity me?
An' winna ye pity my poor steed,
    Stands trembling at yon tree?'

'I wadna pity your poor steed,
    Tho' it were tied to a thorn;
For if ye wad gain my love the night
    Ye wad slight me ere the morn.

'For I ken you by your weel-busked hat,
    And your merrie twinkling ee,
That ye're the laird o' the Oakland hills,
    An' ye may weel seem for to be.'

'But I am not the laird o' the Oakland hills,
    Ye're far mista'en o' me;
But I'm ane o'·the men about his house,
    An' right aft in his companie.'

He's ta'en her by the middle jimp,
    And by the grass-green sleeve,
He's lifted her over the fauld-dyke,
    And speered at her sma' leave.

O he's ta'en out a purse o' gowd,
    And streeked her yellow hair;
'Now take ye that, my bonny may,
    Of me till you hear mair.'

O he's leapt on his berry-brown steed,
    An' soon he's o'er ta'en his men;
And ane and a' cried out to him,
    'O master, ye've tarried lang!'

'O I hae been east, and I hae been west,
    An' I hae been far o'er the knows,
But the bonniest lass that ever I saw
    Is i' the bought, milkin' the ewes.'

She set the cog upon her head,
    An' she's gane singing hame:
'O where hae ye been, my ae daughter?
    Ye hae na been your lane.'

'O nae body was wi' me, father,
    O nae body has been wi' me;
The night is misty and mirk, father,
    Ye may gang to the door and see.

'But wae be to your ewe-herd, father,
    And an ill deed may he die!
He bug the bought at the back o' the know
    And a tod has frightened me.

'There came a tod to the bought-door,
    The like I never saw;
And ere he had taken the lamb he did
    I had lourd he had taken them a'.'

O whan fifteen weeks was come and gane,
    Fifteen weeks and three,
That lassie began to look thin and pale,
    An' to long for his merry-twinkling ee.

It fell on a day, on a het simmer day,
    She was ca'ing out her father s kye,
By came a troop o' gentlemen,
    A' merrilie riding bye.

146

'Weel may ye save an' see, bonny may!
    Weel may ye save and see!
Weel I wat ye be a very bonny may
    But whae's aught that babe ye are wi'?'

Never a word could that lassie say,
    For never a ane could she blame,
An' never a word could the lassie say,
    But, 'I have a good man at hame.'

'Ye lied, ye lied, my very bonny may,
    Sae loud as I hear you lie!
For dinna ye mind that misty night
    I was i' the bought wi' thee?

'I ken you by your middle sae jimp,
    An' your merry-twinkling ee,
That ye're the bonny lass i' the Cowdenknow,
    An' ye may weel seem for to be.'

Than he's leapt off his berry-brown steed,
    An' he's set that fair may on:
'Caw out your kye, gude father, yoursel',
    For she's never caw them out again.

'I am the laird o' the Oakland hills,
    I hae thirty plows and three,
An' I hae gotten the bonniest lass
    That's in the south country.'

# TRUE TAMMAS
## [Child 8B]

Scott's *Minstrelsy* version is 'Erlinton'. 'True Tammas' was recorded
by James Telfer and given to Robert White of Newcastle.

There was a knight, an he had a daughter,
    And he wad wed her, wi' muckle sin;
Sae he has biggit a bonnie bower, love,
    An a' to keep his fair daughter in.

But she hadna been in the bonnie bower, love,
    And no twa hours but barely ane,
Till up started Tammas, her ain true lover,
    And O sae fain as he wad been in.

'For a' sae weel as I like ye, Tammas,
    An for a' sae weel as I like the gin,
I wadna for ten thousand pounds, love,
    Na no this night wad I let thee in.

'But yonder is a bonnie greenwud,
    An in the greenwud there is a wauk,
An I'll be there an sune the morn, love,
    It's a' for my true love's sake.

'On my right hand I'll have a glove, love,
    An on my left ane I'll have nane;
I'll have wi' me my sisters six, love,
    An we will wauk the wuds our lane.'

They hadna waukd the bonnie greenwud,
    Na no an hour but barely ane,
Till up start Tammas, her ain true lover,
    He's ta'en her sisters her frae mang.

An he has kissed her sisters six, love,
    An he has sent them hame again,
But he has keepit his ain true lover,
    Saying, 'We will wauk the wuds our lane.'

They hadna waukd in the bonnie greenwud
    Na no an hour but barely ane,
Till up start fifteen o' the bravest outlaws
    That ever bure either breath or bane.

An up bespak the foremost man, love,
    An O but he spak angrily:
'Either your life – or your lady fair, sir,
    This night shall wauk the wuds wi' me.'

'My lady fair, O I like her weel, sir,
    An O my life, but it lies me near!
But before I lose my lady fair, sir,
    I'll rather lose my life sae dear.'

Then up bespak the second man, love,
    An aye he spak mair angrily,
Saying, 'Baith your life, and your lady fair, sir,
    This night shall wauk the wuds wi' me.'

'My lady fair, O I like her weel, sir,
    An O my life, but it lies me near!
But before I lose my lady fair, sir,
    I'll rather lose my life sae dear.

'But if ye'll be men to your manhood,
    As that I will be unto mine,
I'll fight ye every ane man by man,
    Till the last drop's blude I hae be slain.

'O sit ye down my dearest dearie,
    Sit down and hold my noble steed,
And see that ye never change your cheer
    Until ye see my body bleed.'

He's feughten a' the fifteen outlaws,
    The fifteen outlaws every ane,
He's left naething but the auldest man
    To go and carry the tidings hame.

An he has gane to his dearest dear,
    An he has kissed her cheek and chin,
Saying, 'Thou art mine ain, I have bought thee dear,
    An we will wauk the wuds our lane.'

BALLADS OF THE SUPERNATURAL

# THE YOUNG TAMLANE
*[Child 391]*

Carterhaugh lies at the confluence of Ettrick and Yarrow Waters,
some two miles south-west of Selkirk.


O I forbid ye, maidens a',
    That wear gowd on your hair,
To come or gae by Carterhaugh;
    For young Tamlane is there.

There's nane, that gaes by Carterhaugh,
    But maun leave him a wad;
Either gowd rings, or green mantles,
    Or else their maidenheid.

Now, gowd rings ye may buy, maidens,
    Green mantles ye may spin;
But, gin ye lose your maidenheid,
    Ye'll ne'er get that agen.

But up then spak her, fair Janet,
    The fairest o' a' her kin;
'I'll cum and gang to Carterhaugh,
    And ask nae leave o' him.'

Janet has kilted her green kirtle,
    A little abune her knee;
And she has braided her yellow hair,
    A little abune her bree.

And when she cam to Carterhaugh,
    She gaed beside the well;
And there she fand his steed standing,
    But away was himsell.

She hadna pu'd a red red rose,
    A rose but barely three;
Till up and starts a wee wee man,
    At Lady Janet's knee.

Says – 'Why pu' ye the rose, Janet?
    What gars ye break the tree?
Or why come ye to Carterhaugh,
    Withouten leave o' me?'

Says – 'Carterhaugh it is mine ain;
    My daddie gave it me;
I'll come and gang to Carterhaugh,
    And ask nae leave o' thee.'

He's ta'en her by the milk-white hand,
    Amang the leaves sae green;
And what they did I cannot tell –
    The green leaves were between.

He's ta'en her by the milk-white hand,
    Amang the roses red;
And what they did I cannot say –
    She ne'er returned a maid.

When she cam to her father's ha',
    She looked pale and wan;
They thought she'd dreed some sair sickness,
    Or been wi' some leman.

She didna comb her yellow hair,
    Nor make meikle o' her heid;
And ilka thing, that lady took,
    Was like to be her deid.

It's four-and-twenty ladies fair
    Were playing at the ba';
Janet, the wightest of them anes,
    Was faintest o' them a'.

Four-and-twenty ladies fair
    Were playing at the chess;
And out there cam the fair Janet,
    As green as any grass.

Out and spak an auld gray-headed knight,
    Lay o'er the castle wa' –
'And ever alas! for thee, Janet,
    But we'll be blamed a'!'

'Now haud your tongue, ye auld gray knight!
    And an ill deid may ye die;
Father my bairn on whom I will,
    I'll father nane on thee.'

Out then spak her father dear,
    And he spak meik and mild –
'And ever alas! my sweet Janet,
    I fear ye gae wi' child.'

'And if I be wi' child, father,
    Mysell maun bear the blame;
There's ne'er a knight about your ha'
    Shall hae the bairnie's name.

'And if I be wi' child, father,
    'Twill prove a wondrous birth;
For weel I swear I'm not wi' bairn
    To any man on earth.

'If my love were an earthly knight,
    As he's an elfin gray,
I wadna gie my ain true love
    For nae lord that ye hae.'

She prinked hersell and prinned hersell,
    By the ae light of the moon,
And she's away to Carterhaugh,
    To speak wi' young Tamlane.

And when she cam to Carterhaugh,
    She gaed beside the well;
And there she saw the steed standing,
    But away was himsell.

She hadna pu'd a double rose,
    A rose but only twae,
When up and started young Tamlane,
    Says – 'Lady, thou pu's nae mae!

'Why pu' ye the rose, Janet,
    Within this garden green,
And a' to kill the bonny babe,
    That we got us between?'

'The truth ye'll tell to me, Tamlane;
    A word ye mauna lie;
Gin e'er ye was in haly chapel,
    Or sained in Christentie.'

'The truth I'll tell to thee, Janet,
    A word I winna lie;
A knight me got, and a lady me bore,
    As well as they did thee.

'Randolph, Earl Murray, was my sire,
    Dunbar, Earl March, is thine;
We loved when we were children small,
    Which yet you well may mind.

'When I was a boy just turned of nine,
    My uncle sent for me,
To hunt, and hawk, and ride with him,
    And keep him cumpanie.

'There cam a wind out of the north,
    A sharp wind and a snell;
And a dead sleep cam over me,
    And frae my horse I fell.

'The Queen of Fairies keppit me,
    In yon green hill to dwell;
And I'm a fairy, lyth and limb;
    Fair ladye, view me well.

'Then would I never tire, Janet,
    In Elfish land to dwell,
But aye, at every seven years,
    They pay the teind to hell;
And I am sae fat and fair of flesh,
    I fear 't will be mysell.

'This night is Halloween, Janet,
    The morn is Hallowday,
And gin ye dare your true love win,
    Ye hae nae time to stay.

'The night it is good Halloween,
    When fairy folk will ride,
And they that wad their true-love win,
    At Miles Cross they maun bide.'

'But how shall I thee ken, Tamlane?
    Or how shall I thee knaw,
Amang so many unearthly knights,
    The like I never saw?'

The first company that passes by,
    Say na, and let them gae;
The next company that passes by,
    Say na, and do right sae;
The third company that passes by,
    Then I'll be ane o' thae.

'First let pass the black, Janet,
    And syne let pass the brown,
But grip ye to the milk-white steed,
    And pu' the rider down.

'For I ride on the milk-white steed,
    And aye nearest the town;
Because I was a christened knight,
    They gave me that renown.

'My right hand will be gloved, Janet,
    My left hand will be bare;
And these tokens I gie thee,
    Nae doubt I will be there.

'They'll turn me in your arms, Janet,
    An adder and a snake;
But had me fast, let me not pass,
    Gin ye wad be my maik.

'They'll turn me in your arms, Janet,
    An adder and an ask;
They'll turn me in your arms, Janet,
    A bale that burns fast.

158

'They'll turn me in your arms, Janet,
    A red-hot gad o' airn;
But haud me fast, let me not pass,
    For I'll do you no harm.

'First dip me in a stand o' milk,
    And then in a stand o' water;
But had me fast, let me not pass,
    I'll be your bairn's father.

'And next they'll shape me in your arms
    A tod but and an eel;
But had me fast, nor let me gang,
    As you do love me weel.

'They'll shape me in your arms, Janet,
    A dove but and a swan,
And last they'll shape me in your arms
    A mother-naked man;
Cast your green mantle over me,
    I'll be myself again.'

Gloomy, gloomy, was the night,
    And eiry was the way,
As fair Janet, in her green mantle,
    To Miles Cross she did gae.

About the dead hour o' the night
    She heard the bridles ring,
And Janet was as glad o' that
    As any earthly thing.

And first gaed by the black black steed,
    And then gaed by the brown;
But fast she gript the milk-white steed,
    And pu'd the rider down.

She pu'd him frae the milk-white steed,
    And loot the bridle fa',
And up there raise an erlish cry,
    'He's won amang us a'!'

They shaped him in fair Janet's arms
    An esk but and an adder;
She held him fast in every shape,
    To be her bairn's father.

They shaped him in her arms at last
    A mother-naked man,
She wrapt him in her green mantle,
    And sae her true love wan.

Up then spake the Queen o' the Fairies,
    Out o' a bush o' broom:
'She that has borrowd young Tamlane
    Has gotten a stately groom.'

Up then spake the Queen o' the Fairies,
    Out o' a bush o' rye:
'She's ta'en awa' the bonniest knight
    In a' my cumpanie.

'But had I kennd, Tamlane,' she says,
    'A lady wad borrowd thee
I wad ta'en out thy twa gray een,
    Put in twa een o' tree.

'Had I but kennd, Tamlane,' she says,
    'Before ye came frae hame,
I wad ta'en out your heart o' flesh,
    Put in a heart o' stane.

'Had I but had the wit yestreen
    That I hae coft the day,
I'd paid my kane seven times to hell
    Ere you'd been won away.'

# THE BROOMFIELD HILL

*[Child 43A]*

There was a knight and a lady bright,
    Had a true tryst at the broom;
The ane gaed early in the morning,
    The other in the afternoon.

And aye she sat in her mother's bower door,
    And aye she made her mane,
'O whether should I gang to the Broomfield hill,
    Or should I stay at hame?

'For if I gang to the Broomfield hill,
    My maidenhead is gone;
And if I chance to stay at hame,
    My love will call me mansworn.'

Up then spake a witch woman,
    Ay from the room aboon;
'O ye may gang to the Broomfield hill,
    And yet come maiden hame.

'For when ye gang to the Broomfield hill,
    Ye'll find your love asleep,
With a silver-belt about his head,
    And a broom-cow at his feet.

'Take ye the blossom of the broom,
    The blossom it smells sweet,
And strew it at your true love's head,
    And likewise at his feet.

'Take ye the rings off your fingers,
        Put them on his right hand,
To let him know, when he doth wake,
        His love was at his command.'

She pu'd the broom flower on Hive-hill,
        And strew'd on his white hals bane,
And that was to be wittering true,
        That maiden she had gane.

'O where were ye, my milk-white steed,
        That I hae coft sae dear,
That wadna watch and waken me,
        When there was maiden here?'

'I stamped wi' my foot, master,
        And gar'd my bridle ring;
But na kin' thing wad waken ye,
        Till she was past and gane.'

'And wae betide ye, my gay goss hawk,
        That I did love sae dear,
That wadna watch and waken me,
        When there was maiden here.'

'I clapped wi' my wings, master,
        And aye my bells I rang,
And aye cried, Waken, waken, master,
        Before the ladye gang.'

'But haste and haste, my gude white steed,
        To come the maiden till,
Or a' the birds, of gude green wood,
        Of your flesh shall have their fill.'

'Ye needna burst your good white steed,
　　Wi' racing o'er the howm;
Nae bird flies faster through the wood,
　　Than she fled through the broom.'

# THOMAS THE RHYMER
*[Child 37C]*

There is evidence that Thomas of Erceldoune lived in the thirteenth century in what is now Earlston on the Leader Water. The ruin known as Rhymer's Tower is nearby.

True Thomas lay on Huntlie Bank;
    A ferlie he spied wi' his e'e;
And there he saw a ladye bright
    Come riding down by the Eildon Tree.

Her shirt was o' the grass-green silk,
    Her mantle o' the velvet fine;
At ilka tett of her horse's mane,
    Hang fifty siller bells and nine.

True Thomas he pulled aff his cap,
    And louted low down to his knee,
'All hail, thou mighty Queen of Heaven!
    For thy peer on earth I never did see.'

'O no, O no, Thomas,' she said;
    'That name does not belang to me;
I am but the Queen of fair Elfland,
    That am hither come to visit thee.

'Harp and carp, Thomas,' she said;
    'Harp and carp along wi' me;
And if ye dare to kiss my lips,
    Sure of your body I will be.'

'Betide me weal, betide me woe,
    That weird shall never danton me.'
Syne he has kissed her rosy lips,
    All underneath the Eildon Tree.

'Now ye maun go wi' me,' she said,
'True Thomas, ye maun go wi' me;
And ye maun serve me seven years,
Thro' weal or woe as may chance to be.'

She mounted on her milk-white steed;
She's ta'en true Thomas up behind;
And aye, whene'er her bridle rung,
The steed flew swifter than the wind.

O they rade on, and farther on;
The steed gaed swifter than the wind,
Until they reached a desert wide,
And living land was left behind.

'Light down, light down, now, true Thomas,
And lean your head upon my knee,
Abide and rest a little space,
And I will show you ferlies three.

'O see ye not yon narrow road,
So thick beset with thorns and briers?
That is the path of righteousness,
Though after it but few enquires.

'And see ye not that braid braid road,
That lies across that lily leven?
That is the path of wickedness,
Though some call it the road to heaven,

'And see ye not that bonny road
That winds about the fernie brae?
That is the road to fair Elfland,
Where thou and I this night maun gae.

'But, Thomas, ye maun hold your tongue,
    Whatever ye may hear or see;
For, if you speak word in Elflyn land,
    Ye'll ne'er get back to your ain countrie.'

O they rade on and farther on,
    And they waded through rivers aboon the knee,
And they saw neither sun nor moon,
    But they heard the roaring of the sea.

It was mirk mirk night, and there was nae stern light,
    And they waded through red blude to the knee;
For a' the blude, that's shed on earth,
    Rins through the springs o' that countrie.

Syne they came on to a garden green,
    And she pu'd an apple frae a tree –
'Take this for thy wages, true Thomas;
    It will give thee a tongue that can never lie.'

'My tongue is mine ain,' true Thomas said;
    'A gudely gift ye wad gie to me!
I neither dought to buy nor sell,
    At fair or tryst where I may be.

'I dought neither speak to prince nor peer,
    Nor ask of grace from fair ladye.'
'Now hold thy peace!' the lady said,
    'For as I say, so must it be.'

He has gotten a coat of the even cloth,
    And a pair of shoes of velvet green;
And, till seven years were gane and past,
    True Thomas on earth was never seen.

# THE WEE WEE MAN
## [Child 38C]

Carterhaugh lies at the confluence of Ettrick and Yarrow Waters, some two miles south-west of Selkirk.

'Twas down by Carterhaugh, father,
    I walked beside the wa',
And there I saw a wee wee man,
    The least that e'er I saw.

His legs were skant a shathmont lang;
    Yet umber was his thie;
Between his brows there was ae span,
    And between his shoulders three.

He's ta'en and flung a meikle stane,
    As far as I could see;
I could na, had I been Wallace wight,
    Hae lifted it to my knee.

'O wee wee man, but ye be strang!
    Where may thy dwelling be?'
'It's down beside yon bonny bower;
    Fair lady, come and see.'

On we lap, and away we rade,
    Down to a bonny green;
We lighted down to bait our steed,
    And we saw the fairy queen.

With four and twenty at her back,
    Of ladies clad in green;
Tho the King of Scotland had been there,
    The worst might hae been his queen.

On we lap, and away we rade,
  Down to a bonny ha';
The roof was o' the beaten gowd,
  The floor was of chrystal a'.

And there were dancing on the floor,
  Fair ladies jimp and sma';
But in the twinkling o' an eye,
  They sainted clean awa'.

# THE CRUEL MOTHER
*[Child 20B]*

She sat down below a thorn,
    Fine flowers in the valley,
And there she has her sweet babe born.
    And the green leaves they grow rarely.

Smile na sae sweet, my bonny babe,
    Fine flowers in the valley,
And ye smile sweet, ye'll smile me dead,
    And the green leaves they grow rarely.

She's ta'en out her little penknife,
    Fine flowers in the valley,
And twinned the sweet babe o' its life,
    And the green leaves they grow rarely.

She's howket a grave by the light o' the moon,
    Fine flowers in the valley,
And there she's buried her sweet babe in,
    And the green leaves they grow rarely.

As she was going to the church,
    Fine flowers in the valley,
She saw a sweet babe in the porch,
    And the green leaves they grow rarely.

O sweet babe and thou wert mine,
    Fine flowers in the valley,
I wad cleed thee in the silk so fine,
    And the green leaves they grow rarely.

O mother dear, when I was thine,
    Fine flowers in the valley,
You didna prove to me sae kind,
    And the green leaves they grow rarely.

# CLERK SAUNDERS
*[Minstrelsy]*

Clerk Saunders and may Margaret
    Walked ower yon garden green;
And sad and heavy was the love
    That fell thir twa between.

'A bed, a bed,' Clerk Saunders said,
    'A bed for you and me!'
'Fye na, fye na,' said may Margaret,
    'Till anes we married be.

'For in may come my seven bauld brothers,
    Wi' torches burning bright;
They'll say – "We hae but ae sister,
    And behold she's wi' a knight!"'

'Then take the sword frae my scabbard,
    And slowly lift the pin;
And you may swear, and safe your aith,
    Ye never let Clerk Saunders in.

'And take a napkin in your hand,
    And tie up baith your bonny een;
And you may swear, and safe your aith,
    Ye saw me na since late yestreen.'

It was about the midnight hour,
    When they asleep were laid,
When in and came her seven brothers,
    Wi' torches burning red.

When in and came her seven brothers,
  Wi' torches shining bright;
They said, 'We hae but ae sister,
  And behold her lying with a knight!'

Then out and spake the first o' them,
  'I bear the sword shall gar him die!'
And out and spake the second o' them,
  'His father has nae mair than he!'

And out and spake the third o' them,
  'I wot that they are lovers dear!'
And out and spake the fourth o' them,
  'They hae been in love this mony a year!'

Then out and spake the fifth o' them,
  'It were great sin true love to twain!'
And out and spake the sixth o' them,
  'It were shame to slay a sleeping man!'

Then up and gat the seventh o' them,
  And never a word spake he;
But he has striped his bright brown brand
  Out through Clerk Saunders' fair bodye.

Clerk Saunders he started, and Margaret she turned
  Into his arms as asleep she lay;
And sad and silent was the night
  That was atween thir twae.

And they lay still and sleeped sound,
  Until the day began to daw;
And kindly to him she did say,
  'It is time, true love, you were awa'.'

But he lay still and sleeped sound,
    Albeit the sun began to sheen;
She looked atween her and the wa',
    And dull and drowsie were his een.

Then in and came her father dear,
    Said – 'Let a' your mourning be;
I'll carry the dead corpse to the clay,
    And I'll come back and comfort thee.'

'Comfort weel your seven sons;
    For comforted will I never be:
I ween 'twas neither knave nor loon
    Was in the bower last night wi' me.'

The clinking bell gaed through the town,
    To carry the dead corse to the clay;
And Clerk Saunders stood at may Margaret's window,
    I wot, an hour before the day.

'Are ye sleeping, Margaret?' he says,
    'Or are ye waking presentlie?
Give me my faith and troth again,
    I wot, true love, I gied to thee.'

'Your faith and troth ye sall never get,
    Nor our true love sall never twin,
Until ye come within my bower,
    And kiss me cheik and chin.'

'My mouth it is full cold, Margaret,
    It has the smell, now, of the ground;
And if I kiss thy comely mouth,
    Thy days of life will not be lang.

'O, cocks are crowing a merry midnight,
    I wot the wild fowls are boding day;
Give me my faith and troth again,
    And let me fare me on my way.'

'Thy faith and troth thou sall na get,
    And our true love sall never twin,
Until ye tell what comes of women,
    I wot, who die in strong traivelling?'

'Their beds are made in the heavens high,
    Down at the foot of our good Lord's knee,
Weel set about wi' gillyflowers;
    I wot sweet company for to see.

'O cocks are crowing a merry midnight,
    I wot the wild fowls are boding day;
The psalms of heaven will soon be sung,
    And I, ere now, will be missed away.'

Then she has ta'en a crystal wand,
    And she has stroken her troth thereon,
She has given it him out at the shot-window,
    Wi' mony a sad sigh, and heavy groan.

'I thank ye, Marg'ret; I thank ye Marg'ret;
    And aye I thank ye heartilie;
Gin ever the dead come for the quick,
    Be sure Marg'ret, I'll come for thee.'

It's hosen and shoon, and gown alone,
    She climbed the wall and followed him,
Until she came to the green forest,
    And there she lost the sight o' him.

'Is there ony room at your head, Saunders?
    Is there ony room at your feet?
Or ony room at your side, Saunders,
    Where fain, fain, I wad sleep?'

'There's nae room at my head, Marg'ret,
    There's nae room at my feet;
My bed it is full lowly now:
    Amang the hungry worms I sleep.

'Cauld mould is my covering now,
    But and my winding sheet;
The dew it falls nae sooner down,
    Than my resting-place is weet.

'But plait a wand o' bonnie birk,
    And lay it on my breast;
And shed a tear upon my grave,
    And wish my saul gude rest.

'And fair Marg'ret, and rare Marg'ret,
    And Marg'ret o' veritie,
Gin e'er ye love another man
    Ne'er love him as ye did me.'

Then up and crew the milk-white cock,
    And up and crew the gray;
Her lover vanished in the air,
    And she gaed weeping away.

# PROUD LADY MARGARET
## [Child 47A]

'Twas on a night, an evening bright,
    When the dew began to fa',
Lady Margaret was walking up and down,
    Looking o'er her castle wa'.

She looked east, and she looked west,
    To see what she could spy,
When a gallant knight came in her sight,
    And to the gate drew nigh,

'You seem to be no gentleman,
    You wear your boots so wide;
But you seem to be some cunning hunter,
    You wear the horn so syde.'

'I am no cunning hunter,' he said,
    'Nor e'er intend to be;
But I am come to this castle
    To seek the love of thee;
And if you do not grant me love,
    This night for thee I'll die.'

'If you should die for me, sir knight,
    There's few for you will mane,
For mony a better has died for me,
    Whose graves are growing green.

'But ye maun read my riddle,' she said,
    'And answer my questions three;
And but ye read them right,' she said,
    'Gae stretch ye out and die. –

'Now what is the flower, the ae first flower,
    Springs either on moor or dale?
And what is the bird, the bonnie bonnie bird,
    Sings on the evening gale?'

'The primrose is the ae first flower,
    Springs either on moor or dale;
And the thristlecock is the bonniest bird,
    Sings on the evening gale.'

'But what's the little coin,' she said,
    'Wald buy my castle bound?
And what's the little boat,' she said,
    'Can sail the world all round?'

'O hey, how many small pennies
    Make thrice three thousand pound?
Or hey, how mony small fishes
    Swim a' the salt sea round?'

'I think ye maun be my match,' she said,
    'My match and something mair;
You are the first e'er got the grant
    Of love from my father's heir.

'My father was lord of nine castles,
    My mother lady of three;
My father was lord of nine castles,
    And there's nane to heir but me.

'And round about a' thae castles,
    You may baith plow and saw,
And on the fifteenth day of May,
    The meadows they will maw.'

'O hald your tongue, Lady Margaret,' he said,
　'For loud I hear you lie!
Your father was lord of nine castles,
　Your mother was lady of three;
Your father was lord of nine castles,
　But ye fa' heir to but three.

'And round about a' thae castles,
　You may baith plow and saw,
But on the fifteenth day of May
　The meadows will not maw.

'I am your brother Willie,' he said,
　'I trow ye ken na me;
I came to humble your haughty heart,
　Has gar'd sae mony die.'

'If ye be my brother Willie,' she said,
　'As I trow weel ye be,
This night I'll neither eat nor drink,
　But gae alang wi' thee.'

'O hold your tongue, Lady Margaret,' he said,
　'Again I hear you lie;
For ye've unwashen hands, and ye've unwashen feet,
　To gae to clay wi' me.

'For the wee worms are my bedfellows,
　And cauld clay is my sheets;
And when the stormy winds do blow,
　My body lies and sleeps.'

# THE WIFE OF USHER'S WELL
## [Child 79A]

There lived a wife at Usher's Well,
    And a wealthy wife was she;
She had three stout and stalwart sons,
    And sent them o'er the sea.

They hadna been a week from her,
    A week but barely ane,
Whan word came to the carline wife,
    That her three sons were gane.

They hadna been a week from her,
    A week but barely three,
Whan word came to the carline wife,
    That her sons she'd never see.

'I wish the wind may never cease,
    Nor fishes in the flood,
Till my three sons come hame to me,
    In earthly flesh and blood!'

It fell about the Martinmas,
    Whan nights are lang and mirk,
The carline wife's three sons came hame,
    And their hats were o' the birk.

It neither grew in syke nor ditch,
    Nor yet in ony sheugh;
But at the gates o' Paradise,
    That birk grew fair eneugh.

\*

179

'Blow up the fire, my maidens!
    Bring water from the well!
For a' my house shall feast this night,
    Since my three sons are well.'

And she has made to them a bed,
    She's made it large and wide;
And she's ta'en her mantle her about,
    Sat down at the bed-side.

\*

Up then crew the red red cock,
    And up and crew the gray;
The eldest to the youngest said,
    'Tis time we were away.'

The cock he hadna crawed but once,
    And clapped his wings at a',
When the youngest to the eldest said,
    'Brother, we must awa'.

The cock doth craw, the day doth daw,
    The channerin' worm doth chide;
Gin we be mist out o' our place,
    A sair pain we maun bide.

'Fare ye weel, my mother dear!
    Fareweel to barn and byre!
And fare ye weel, the bonny lass,
    That kindles my mother's fire.'

# YOUNG BENJIE
### [Child 86A]


Of a' the maids o' fair Scotland,
    The fairest was Marjorie;
And young Benjie was her ae true love,
    And a dear true love was he.

And wow! but they were lovers dear,
    And loved fu' constantlie;
But aye the mair when they fell out,
    The sairer was their plea,

And they hae quarrelled on a day,
    Till Marjorie's heart grew wae;
And she said she'd chuse another luve,
    And let young Benjie gae.

And he was stout, and proud-hearted,
    And thought o't bitterlie;
And he's gaen by the wan moonlight,
    To meet his Marjorie.

'O open, open, my true love,
    O open, and let me in!'
'I dare na open, young Benjie,
    My three brothers are within.'

'Ye lied, ye lied, ye bonny burd,
    Sae loud's I hear ye lie;
As I came by the Lowden banks,
    They bade gude e'en to me.

'But fare ye weel, my ae fause love,
    That I have loved sae lang!
It sets ye chuse another love,
    And let young Benjie gang.'

Then Marjorie turned her round about,
    The tear blinding her e'e, –
'I darena, darena, let thee in,
    But I'll come down to thee.'

Then saft she smiled, and said to him,
    'O what ill hae I done?'
He took her in his armis twa,
    And threw her o'er the linn.

The stream was strang, the maid was stout,
    And laith laith to be dang,
But, ere she wan the Lowden banks,
    Her fair colour was wan.

Then up bespak her eldest brother,
    'O see na ye what I see?'
And out then spak her second brother,
    'It's our sister Marjorie!'

Out then spak her eldest brother,
    'O how shall we her ken?'
And out then spak her youngest brother,
    'There's a honey mark on her chin.'

Then they've ta'en up the comely corpse,
    And laid it on the ground –
'O wha has killed our ae sister,
    And how can he be found?

'The night it is her low lykewake,
    The morn her burial day,
And we maun watch at mirk midnight,
    And hear what she will say.'

Wi' doors ajar, and candle light,
    And torches burning clear;
The streikit corpse, till still midnight,
    They waked, but naething hear.

About the middle o' the night,
    The cocks began to craw;
And at the dead hour o' the night,
    The corpse began to thraw.

'O whae has done thee wrang, sister,
    Or dared the deadly sin?
Whae was sae stout, and feared nae dout,
    As thraw ye o'er the linn?'

'Young Benjie was the first ae man
    I had my love upon;
He was sae stout, and proud-hearted,
    He threw me o'er the linn.'

'Sall we young Benjie head, sister,
    Sall we young Benjie hang;
Or sall we pike out his twa grey een,
    And punish him ere he gang?'

'Ye mauna Benjie head, brothers,
    Ye mauna Benjie hang,
But ye maun pike out his twa grey een,
    And punish him ere he gang.

'Tie a green gravat round his neck,
    And lead him out and in,
And the best ae servant about your house
    To wait young Benjie on.

'And ay, at every seven years' end,
    Ye'll tak him to the linn;
For that's the penance he maun drie,
    To scug his deadly sin.'

| | | | |
|---|---|---|---|
| *ablins* | perhaps | *caugers:* | carriers, hucksters |
| *abune* | above | *cauler* | fresh |
| *aevery* | voracious | *cawte* | wary |
| *agayne* | in reply | *channerin'* | fretting |
| *airn(s)* | iron(s) | *clam* | climbed |
| *airt* | direction | *cleed* | clothed |
| *ask; esk* | newt | *clock* | hobbler |
| | | *clouted* | patched |
| *basnet* | helmet | *cog* | milk-pail |
| *batts* | beating | *collayne* | Cologne steel |
| *berne* | man | *corbie* | crow |
| *beseen* | appointed | *corse* | cross |
| *biggit* | built | *courtrie* | courtiers |
| *billie* | friend; brother | *cowte* | colt |
| *birst* | battle | *crouse* | conceit |
| *black mail* | protection money | *cumber* | tumult |
| *bor(r)ow* | ransom | *curch* | kerchief |
| *bought; bucht* | fold; pen | | |
| *bound; bowyn* | ready | *danton* | daunt |
| *branks* | halter | *den* | dene; glen |
| *brayd* | press | *dought* | was able |
| *brecham* | horse collar | *dow* | can |
| *broken men* | outlaws | *dowie* | melancholy |
| *broomcow* | twig of broom | *drede* | doubt |
| *buft coat* | leather jacket | *dree; drie* | suffer |
| *bug* | built | *drifts* | flocks |
| *burd* | maiden | *dung* | defeated |
| *busked* | decorated | | |
| *but and* | and also | *elshin* | awl |
| *by* | besides | *eme* | uncle |
| | | *envye* | harm |
| *carl(e)* | old man | | |
| *carline* | old woman | *fail dyke* | turf wall |

185

*fang*   catch
*fankit*   entangled
*fauld*   fold
*feid*   feud
*feiries*   comrades
*ferlies*   marvels
*fie; fey*   predestined
*fit(ted)*   foot(ed)
*fley(e)d*   frightened
*flinders*   splinters
*forehammer*   large hammer
   which strikes before the
   smaller
*forfaulted*   forfeited
*forfoughen*   exhausted
*fou*   drunk; full
*freke*   warrior
*frith*   wood; enclosed land
*fylde*   chance

*gad*   bar
*gait*   goat
*gar*   cause; compel
*gaun*   going
*gear*   goods
*genzie*   engine of war
*gi'en*   given
*gilt*   money; gilded
*gin*   if
*gleed*   glowing ember
*goud*   gold
*graithed*   clothed in armour
*green*   long for
*greet*   weep
*gryming*   thin covering

*ha'*   hall

*ha(u)d:*   hold
*hail*   whole
*ha(u)ld*   stronghold; pele
*hause*   neck
*hente*   caught
*herry*   pillage
*het*   hot
*howm*   holm; river meadow
*houp; hope*   hill slope
*hyght*   promised

*ilk ane*   every one
*insight (gear)*   household
   goods

*jack*   reinforced jacket
*jaw*   wave
*jimp*   slender

*kane*   rent in kind
*kinnen*   rabbits
*kirn*   churn
*knapscap*   steel bonnet
*knee-pan*   knee-cap
*know(e)*   hillock
*kythed*   appeared

*land-sergeant*   warden's
   deputy
*lave*   the rest
*lawing*   reckoning
*layne*   lie
*leal*   loyal
*lear*   learning; information
*lee*   waste
*leugh*   laughed
*leven*   lawn

186

| | | | |
|---|---|---|---|
| *lidder* | lazy | *pallions* | pavilions; tents |
| *lightly* | slight | *pick* | pitch |
| *lily lee* | lovely bank | *plat* | entwined |
| *linn* | waterfall | *plea* | dispute |
| *lirk* | hollow | *plummet* | pommel |
| *loan* | lane | *pure* | poor |
| *loot* | allowed | *pype (of wine)* | 100 gallons |
| *loup* | leap | | |
| *lourd* | rather | *quey* | heifer |
| *low* | flame | | |
| *lucettes* | pikes | *rad* | afraid |
| *lyart* | grey | *ramp* | wild |
| *lyth* | joint | *ranshackle* | ransack |
| | | *ray* | track |
| *mair* | more; again | *red* | clear away; stop |
| *make* | mate | *reif* | robbery |
| *mansworn* | perjured | *reiver* | robber |
| *marrow* | mate | *rig* | ridge |
| *maunna* | must not | *roke* | vapour |
| *maut* | malt; ale | *rout* | bellow |
| *may* | maiden | *row* | rough |
| *mergh* | marrow | *rowghte* | company; men |
| *mese* | soothe | *ryall* | royal |
| *mickle* | great; much | | |
| *mind* | remember; remind | *saftly* | softly |
| *minnie* | mother | *sained* | blessed |
| *mirk* | dark | *sainted* | vanished |
| | | *sark* | shirt |
| *nagie* | pony | *scug* | expiate |
| *neist* | next | *seld* | sold |
| *nogs* | notches; stakes | *shathmont* | six inches |
| | | *sheugh* | hollow |
| *or* | ere; before | *sicker* | safe |
| *ousen* | oxen | *skaith* | hurt |
| *outspeckle* | laughing stock | *slight* | reduce; demolish |
| *ower-word* | repeated cry | *slogan* | battle-cry |

187

slough-hound    blood-hound
Soudron    Southron; English
spauld    shoulder
speer    ask
splent    armour of
    overlapping plates
staig    young stallion
stark    strong
stawn    stolen
stear    stir
stot    young ox
stounde    time
stoure    strife
stout    haughty
styll    secretly
syde    low down
syke    bog
syne    then; afterwards

targats    tassels
teind    tithe
the tone    one
thir    these
thraw    throw; twist
tide    time
tint    lost
to-name    nickname
toom    empty

traivelling    childbirth
trew; true    trow; believe
twa(e)    two
twin'd    separated

umber    massive
upgive    surrender

wache    sentinel
wad    would
wad    wager
wae    sorrowful
wan    won; got
wap    lap; twine
wat    know
I wat    indeed
water-gate    river path
weel    well
weil sped    successful
weir    war
whang    thong
wicker    twig; rod
wight    strong
winne    joy
wittering    hint
won    live
wood    mad

yate; yett    gate; door

# Fyfield*Books*

*Two millennia of essential classics*

The extensive Fyfield*Books* list includes

**Djuna Barnes** *The Book of Repulsive Women and other poems*
edited by Rebecca Loncraine

**Elizabeth Barrett Browning** *Selected Poems* edited by Malcolm Hicks

**Charles Baudelaire** *Complete Poems in French and English*
translated by Walter Martin

**Thomas Lovell Beddoes** *Death's Jest-Book* edited by Michael Bradshaw

**Aphra Behn** *Selected Poems*
edited by Malcolm Hicks

*Border Ballads: A Selection*
edited by James Reed

**The Brontë Sisters** *Selected Poems*
edited by Stevie Davies

**Sir Thomas Browne** *Selected Writings*
edited by Claire Preston

**Lewis Carroll** *Selected Poems*
edited by Keith Silver

**Paul Celan** *Collected Prose*
translated by Rosmarie Waldrop

**Thomas Chatterton** *Selected Poems*
edited by Grevel Lindop

**John Clare** *By Himself*
edited by Eric Robinson and David Powell

**Arthur Hugh Clough** *Selected Poems*
edited by Shirley Chew

**Samuel Taylor Coleridge** *Selected Poetry* edited by William Empson and David Pirie

**Tristan Corbière** *The Centenary Corbière*
*in French and English*
translated by Val Warner

**William Cowper** *Selected Poems*
edited by Nick Rhodes

**Gabriele d'Annunzio** *Halcyon*
translated by J.G. Nichols

**John Donne** *Selected Letters*
edited by P.M. Oliver

**William Dunbar** *Selected Poems*
edited by Harriet Harvey Wood

**Anne Finch, Countess of Winchilsea** *Selected Poems*
edited by Denys Thompson

**Ford Madox Ford** *Selected Poems*
edited by Max Saunders

**John Gay** *Selected Poems*
edited by Marcus Walsh

**Oliver Goldsmith** *Selected Writings*
edited by John Lucas

**Robert Herrick** *Selected Poems*
edited by David Jesson-Dibley

**Victor Hugo** *Selected Poetry*
*in French and English*
translated by Steven Monte

**T.E. Hulme** *Selected Writings*
edited by Patrick McGuinness

**Leigh Hunt** *Selected Writings*
edited by David Jesson Dibley

**Wyndham Lewis** *Collected Poems and Plays* edited by Alan Munton

**Charles Lamb** *Selected Writings*
edited by J.E. Morpurgo

**Lucretius** *De Rerum Natura: The Poem on Nature*
translated by C.H. Sisson

John Lyly *Selected Prose and Dramatic Work*
edited by Leah Scragg

Ben Jonson *Epigrams and The Forest*
edited by Richard Dutton

Giacomo Leopardi *The Canti*
*with a selection of his prose*
translated by J.G. Nichols

Stéphane Mallarmé *For Anatole's Tomb*
*in French and English*
translated by Patrick McGuinness

Andrew Marvell *Selected Poems*
edited by Bill Hutchings

Charlotte Mew *Collected Poems and Selected Prose*
edited by Val Warner

Michelangelo *Sonnets*
translated by Elizabeth Jennings,
introduction by Michael Ayrton

William Morris *Selected Poems*
edited by Peter Faulkner

John Henry Newman *Selected Writings to 1845*
edited by Albert Radcliffe

Ovid *Amores*
translated by Tom Bishop

Fernando Pessoa *A Centenary Pessoa*
edited by Eugenio Lisboa and L.C.
Taylor, introduction by Octavio Paz

Petrarch *Canzoniere*
translated by J.G. Nichols

Edgar Allan Poe *Poems and Essays on Poetry*
edited by C.H. Sisson

*Restoration Bawdy*
edited by John Adlard

Rainer Maria Rilke *Sonnets to Orpheus and Letters to a Young Poet*
translated by Stephen Cohn

Christina Rossetti *Selected Poems*
edited by C.H. Sisson

Dante Gabriel Rossetti *Selected Poems and Translations*
edited by Clive Wilmer

Sir Walter Scott *Selected Poems*
edited by James Reed

Sir Philip Sidney *Selected Writings*
edited by Richard Dutton

John Skelton *Selected Poems*
edited by Gerald Hammond

Charlotte Smith *Selected Poems*
edited by Judith Willson

Henry Howard, Earl of Surrey *Selected Poems*
edited by Dennis Keene

Algernon Charles Swinburne *Selected Poems*
edited by L.M. Findlay

Arthur Symons *Selected Writings*
edited by Roger Holdsworth

William Tyndale *Selected Writings*
edited by David Daniell

Oscar Wilde *Selected Poems*
edited by Malcolm Hicks

William Wordsworth *The Earliest Poems* edited by Duncan Wu

Sir Thomas Wyatt *Selected Poems*
edited by Hardiman Scott

For more information, including a full list of Fyfield*Books* and a contents list for each title, and details of how to order the books in the UK, visit the Fyfield website at www.fyfieldbooks.co.uk or email info@fyfieldbooks.co.uk. For information about Fyfield*Books* available in the United States and Canada, visit the Routledge website at www.routledge-ny.com.